# The Effective Strategist

## Key Skills for all Managers

John van Maurik

Gower

Published by
Gower Publishing Limited
Gower House
Croft Road
Aldershot
Hampshire GU11 3HR
England

Gower
Old Post Road
Brookfield
Vermont 05036
USA

British Library Cataloguing in Publication Data
Van Maurik, John
    The effective strategist : key skills for all managers
    1. Strategic planning
    I. Title
    658.4'012

    ISBN 0–566–08044–3

Typeset in Times by IML Typographers, Chester and printed in Great Britain by MPG Books Ltd, Bodmin.

# Contents

# The Effective Strategist

# Acknowledgements

I would like to thank Gavin Barrett, Rupert Eales-White, Philip Foster and Keith Niblett for their help, material and encouragement.

*John van Maurik*

# Chapter 1

# What is strategy?

Strategy is an elusive concept. People refer to business or military strategies, they praise leaders for being strategic or denigrate them for not having any observable strategies but seldom do they define the word in a way that makes it understandable, available to the majority and a tool that can help both individuals and businesses to grow, expand and meet the demands of an ever-changing world.

So, before this book goes any further it is necessary to make one thing perfectly clear – strategy is not something that is reserved exclusively for those at the top of business, the armed forces or government. Indeed, Michael Porter, one of the most respected writers on the subject, said:

> Strategy is not just for top managers, the best companies are those where everybody lives the strategy to make up low-cost or unique products or services.

To further emphasise this theme, being strategic is something that we all can be, must be and in fact are – if only we knew it! This comes about by virtue of our common humanity; in fact it is easier to be strategic than it is to be a leader. However, like being a leader, being strategic is something that most regard as being the territory of other people – the so called 'strategic thinkers'!

A common reason why most people do not believe that they are strategic, or that they are capable of implementing strategies, is simply because they do not understand what strategy is. The word is cloaked in mystery and what makes it worse is that most attempts to clarify it have served only to deepen the confusion. Here are some of the worst examples of strategic jargon which, when taken out of context, are enough to put off even the hardiest student.

- Criteria for market effectiveness
- Stretch and leverage
- Core competency diagnosis
- SBU versus core competencies
- Positioning
- Competitive position matrix

- ● SWOT analysis
- ● et cetera, et cetera

The jargon is almost endless but I am loath to expand any further for fear of totally alienating the reader at this early stage! Suffice it to say, the above are all valid and useful concepts, but unless taken in the context of what strategy *really* is are both useless and dangerous! If you have ever stopped to plan a holiday, think about your career, analyse how to advance a relationship with an attractive member of the opposite sex or taken steps to buy a house, then you have acted strategically.

But at this stage it is necessary to start to build up a coherent picture of what strategy really is and this will be done via a series of contrasting definitions, at the end of which we will focus on one clear definition which will then be used as the model and framework for further thoughts about strategy within this book.

## A cornucopia of definitions

The word strategy is derived from 'Strategia – the art of war', a term used by the ancient Greeks to describe the exploits of some of their more illustrious generals. Indeed, it was the bravery, determination, but above all the excellent military minds of heroes such as Alexander the Great that altered the geography of the old world and set powerful examples for military thinking for centuries to come. And so, initially, the concept of strategy was firmly rooted in the art of war. Other more modern definitions compounded this mindset. The *Oxford English Dictionary* defines strategy as 'The art of a commander in chief; the art of projecting and directing the larger military movements and operations of a campaign'. It later goes on to talk about the study of strategy as 'the art of bringing forces into contact with the enemy' and then of tactics, which it states 'is the art of using those forces when they are in contact with the enemy'. In his famous treatise on war, von Clausewitz elaborated on this theme by stating that 'Strategy has in its first instance only the victory, that is, the tactical result, as a means to its object.'

And so, the concept of strategy became clearly rooted as a military tool, a means for enabling people with a clear objective to reach it in a purposeful and effective manner. Another definition of strategy is 'The art of having the right people and assets in the right place in order to win. To do so needs a long-term plan. Tactics are short-term plans and initiatives and the means adapted to carry them out.' Looking at these definitions, it is easy to see how military strategy has been used to achieve clear-cut aims and objectives in a multitude of military scenarios. For example, in the Second World War the British side of the D-Day campaign for the Normandy invasion involved the deployment of over one million service personnel, supplies amounting to 20m rounds of artillery ammunition, 2.8m tons of petrol, 324 000 vehicles, 41m cigarettes, 4m magazines, 1.2m books and 8m bandages. In addition, a gigantic transport operation was implemented involving the landing of 1076 locomotives, the rebuilding of 91 bridges and the quarrying of 2m tonnes of stone.

A gigantic strategic operation made more complex by the need to co-ordinate the operation of different armies. By contrast, in the First World War, where, as it has often been argued, there was total confusion between tactics and strategy, the whole situation quite literally became bogged down. The result was a massive cost in human lives.

Later definitions, however, have moved the concept of strategy forward and out of the restrictions of its military heritage. A more modern statement from *Collins Dictionary* describes it as 'A long-term plan for success, especially in politics, business and war'. This is getting better, is more relevant but still misses some essential questions about the subject such as:

● Where does it come from?
● How is it achieved?
● Why should long-term plans be so important?
● Who should create the strategies?

These, as we shall see later, are all in themselves questions of a strategic nature. But first it is necessary to examine why it is so vital for individuals to think strategically about something, which in turn should enable actions to take place which make both their organizations more profitable as well as better places to work.

## The rise of strategy

A brief overview of the twentieth century indicates a steady increase in the amount of strategic thinking taking place, as well as, more recently, a change in the circumstances governing business, politics and careers that not only increases the need for strategies but also renders many of the traditional methods of strategic planning obsolescent.

In the 1930s and 1940s, thanks to early management gurus such as Taylor and Sloan, a phenomenon known as scientific management grew in the US. Elsewhere, Fascist planning began to transform Germany and Italy while in the USSR, Soviet economic planning began to transform the country from a feudal Tsarist economy to something debatably less effective and more sinister. During the Second World War there were many examples showing that integrated planning could work; the US produced more food than it needed while the UK was forced to ration it; yet the fruits of the integrated planning and objectives became evident as the convoy system saved the country from starvation.

In the 1950s and 1960s Keynesian-style planning was in vogue and in the mid-1960s the British Labour Government initiated a five-year economic plan. At the same time a huge increase in the number of consulting organizations specializing in strategy took place; the future was now thought to be foreseeable. In the confidence of the early 1960s many old certainties about life and the nature of the *status quo* flourished brightly before being extinguished for ever – the US inconceivably was to lose the Vietnam war, the UK was to be plunged into a three-day working week, oil prices were to soar as part of the OPEC crisis and two dark new phenomena were to emerge: international terrorism and AIDS. Suddenly the future was not so easy to plan or predict but the need to make some sense out of the growing chaos was stronger than ever.

And so it is in the light of these unpredictable yet accelerating changes that we start to look at the concept of strategy and, more importantly, the ability to think strategically along with the mindset that this itself entails. But first, in order to put the need for strategic thinking into clearer context, it is necessary to look more closely at the creeping chaos, as some may see it, or the widening field of opportunity, as others may perceive it, before reaching the definition of strategy and strategic thought processes that will prevail in this book.

## The changing economic, political and business environments

As individuals, we are locked in. There are pressures and forces at work in the world that will affect all of our lives. Conceivably, one could become a hermit and live in a cave on some remote island in order to avoid the pressures of the new millennium. Possibly you might succeed in avoiding them, but I would not bet on it. The tide is running too powerfully, there is an irresistible pull towards something new. But what?

Pundits ranging from Erasmus through to Alvin Toffler and Bob Dylan have voiced their predictions about the future and the speed of change. They may have different perspectives, but on one thing they all agree. The future is coming and it is coming fast. You had better be ready for it!

So, perhaps at this stage we need to stop the clock and take a rain check. Where are we now? What are the overall political, geographical and economic forces that are affecting the world in which we live? What then are the allied, but different, forces that are influencing the world of business, the world that governs our working lives and potential prosperity?

In stopping the clock, there are dangers. Times move on fast and what may seem significant at the time of writing may appear commonplace at the time of publication. Nevertheless, there are some mega situations that logically could be expected to influence the globe for some decades to come. In naming them, however, I am in no way attempting to make forecasts of an economic or social nature – therein lies madness! For example, here is an early attempt at forecasting. In 1890, Victorian planners attempted to predict what London would be like in 1950. They reached the conclusion that horse-drawn traffic would have overwhelmed the city. The stench of horse dung would make living in the metropolis unbearable, there would be a massive over-supply of fertilizer and there would be no unemployment (presumably every able-bodied person would have been employed in the disposal of horse manure!).

So forecasting is dangerous; statistical trends can be invalidated by the unpredictability of nature and mankind – but, if we stop to examine where we are now, then certain questions concerning where we are going appear inevitable.

So, where are we now?

A brief look at some of the more lasting ongoing situations around the globe may stimulate further questions about the future. On examination, it would appear that just about every economy and society is in a state of transition. The former USSR now has deep social and political problems; the decline of a powerful central government has given rise to a fraught range of internal instabilities ranging from major uprisings in Kazakhstan to less obvious bids for autonomy. This has resulted in the resources of large parts of the former Soviet Union not being fully exploited. In addition, a decline in the rule of law together with a disrespect for the accepted rules governing international business contracts has acted as a brake on overseas investment. Put this together with overall poor economic performance, huge international debts, the rise of a vicious internal mafia coupled with business adventurism; add a further spicy ingredient – the decay of the once all-powerful nuclear power (a phenomenon that has resulted in a bored, unpaid navy sitting on top of a vast citadel of rusting nuclear hardware) – and we have an explosive recipe.

Central Europe is also interesting. Several of the northern states, such as Hungary, Poland, Czechoslovakia and East Germany, have successfully broken free of the thrall of Communism and are developing fast. The situation is, however, different in the southern states. Bulgaria and Roumania have not yet fully embraced reform while Albania has become a byword for poverty. And then there are the Balkan states – Serbia, Croatia and Bosnia – locked into ethnic hatred, having shattered their cities with shelling, murdered their own people and poisoned their beautiful countryside with literally millions of land mines – each of which will cost somebody £2000 to dispose of at some time in the future!

Then there is Asia – the region of the tiger economies. Suppliers of competitively priced electronic goods and vehicles that threaten to further obliterate so many more Western industries, and where the threat has been that they could produce equal – or higher – quality goods with wage bills of under 20 per cent of those carried by Western organizations. But have the tigers lost their teeth? What exactly is going on and how will the new uncertainties in the East affect the rest of the world? In many economies, the culture has been that of authoritarianism with top-down, export-led growth directed by governments that have dictated everything from how business is done to acceptable behaviour in the street. This has also usually been coupled with a system of learning by rote that has stifled creativity at the primary school stage, leaving these burgeoning economies populated with workers who are less able to deal with the next stage of their development. For example, if future development is to be about innovative uses of information technology, exploitation of individual creativity, increasing decentralization and the need to value differences, then the cracks which have already appeared may run deeper than anyone has yet imagined.

These cracks are noticeable in further examining some of South-east Asia's issues. Singapore is facing rising costs and both population and innovation shortages; Malaysia is predicting a shortage of skilled workers; the Philippines are hampered by poor infrastructure, while Indonesia, seen by some as the nation with the greatest potential in the region, is becoming hampered by corruption and protectionism. Throughout the region, growth has in the past been dramatic, bringing prosperity to many. But now even some of the pessimists are wondering whether they underrated the extent of the problems. Dr Mahathir, Prime Minister of Malaysia, stated publicly that the worst was yet to come and at the time he may have been wondering just as much what to do with the large numbers of immigrant workers in his country, for whom there were now no jobs, as what to do about the international currency speculators whom he considered had undermined his country's economy. One thing certainly is true – South-east Asian countries are competing with each other to export to the West and export prices are dropping while unemployment is rising. More than one financial institution has fallen and a new emotion is prevalent – uncertainty.

At the 1998 Strategic Leadership Conference in New York, Chris Patten, ex-Governor of Hong Kong, emphasized that it was going to be tough for the East, with the possible exception of Hong Kong, if the ex-colony could make the most of the legacy of the stability of its Western institutions, coupled with the potential might of the burgeoning Chinese economy. But in reality, no one is quite sure how either Hong Kong or the West would cope with a total economic collapse in the Far East.

Finally, there is what may still be called the 'First World'; although for how much longer? At the time of writing the US is riding the wave of an economic boom; many of the tensions of the 1960s and 1970s are far less apparent. Can it continue? What are the implications of the decline of English as the first language in many parts of the country? For example, try catching a taxi in New York and your driver will probably prefer you to speak Arabic, or especially Spanish. Try getting around in Southern California and Spanish will certainly be more useful than English. Then what about the growing underclass, a phenomenon that has transcended ethnic origin?

In the UK there are a number of powerful forces at work. Many of these concern the country's very identity, its own view of itself. There are crucial issues of sovereignty in relation to the European Parliament to be resolved; coupled to this is the question of a common currency and the impact on economic freedom. Put this together with the question of the devolution of power to Wales and Scotland, a process that could result in the eventual break-up of the Union, add a growing dissatisfaction with the concept of monarchy and you have the ingredients for considerable uncertainty. Then consider the soaring crime rate, much of it based on the growing drug culture, something that has made many a British city far more dangerous than the erstwhile notorious New York, and you may have the makings of a situation that even the famous British stoicism may not be able to endure!

This analysis may seem gloomy, it may seem unusually threatening; indeed, it will probably have been fully overtaken by events by the time it is read and you may well smile and shake your head at some of its misconceptions. Nevertheless, in looking at each geographical situation a number of questions arose and, as will be seen later, they play a vital part in the creation of any strategy. Furthermore, both the issues and the questions have a direct bearing on the factors governing the changing business environment – the place where so many of today's strategies are born.

# Issues facing business

Paradoxically, many of the factors affecting the business environment are less volatile than those influencing the global, economic, social and political scenes; they are, however, influenced by them and cannot be considered in isolation from them. However, when we examine the factors that contribute to the nature of the ever-changing business environment, it is easy to see how a management board or an individual could be wrong-footed if they do not take account of them in their thinking about the way that the business should develop.

The key changes that are impacting on the business environment can be summarized as follows:

*Technological*
As will be seen later, technology is moving forward at a phenomenal rate, challenging not only the way in which we do business and process information but also our ethics, morals and the way we think about life. The rate of change will gather momentum and both the challenges as well as the benefits can only increase.

*Globalization*
Malpractice in an obscure nuclear power plant pollutes half the northern hemisphere – the move to the global village proceeds at a gallop *mainly* as a result of the technological revolution. Both the threats as well as the opportunities are awesome.

*Deregulation*
Following the 'Big Bang' in the City of London in the 1980s, many of the 'sacred cows' of regulation and separation of business practices have been led to the slaughterhouse. In the UK, building societies, a bastion of traditional practice, have been shedding their mutual status, tempting their members with lucrative share options, and even in the legal world several borders are being breached.

*Political and economic*
National boundaries are coming down. In Europe the European Union (EU) will inevitably change the way in which governments and individuals think about their finances, their fiscal systems and the way in which they regulate the activities of businesses and individuals. In turn, a whole range of new legislative measures face those involved in business. It is ironic that much of the debate over Britain's membership of the EU has been over the Social Chapter – a series of legislative measures which are designed to protect the employment of individuals but which, it is alleged, has so mitigated against the rights of employers that in some EU countries organizations avoid taking on permanent staff, thereby frustrating the basic purpose of the law.

*Social and demographic*
Attitudes to work change as does the structure and make-up of society; both people

and skills cross boundaries. In recruiting its workforce, an organization must take a number of new factors into account, secure in the knowledge that what is recommended today will probably become law tomorrow.

### Environmental

The protection of the environment remains an issue although it has not yet received the total protection of law that it deserves. That time will come and the political correctness of being environmentally friendly must eventually overtake other political correctnesses governing race, ability and gender as the effects of irresponsible attitudes towards the planet reach the doors of legislators and fat cats alike.

The implications of these changes to the overall business environment can be summarized as follows:

- There will be increasing levels of uncertainty brought on by accelerating change coupled with fewer definitive answers to the resultant dilemmas.

- However, there will be more opportunity to succeed and an increasing level of choice in how to do so. At the same time, with increasing opportunity, as ever comes a growing range of risks.

- Some of the risk will come in the form of new competitors, overseas competitors and intensifying competition from sources previously not considered.

- As a result, there will be a far higher level of business failures while at the same time the amount of takeovers, mergers and acquisitions will soar. In many respects this is already well under way. In *Thriving on Chaos* (1987), Tom Peters looked back at the companies he had used as examples in *In Search of Excellence* (1982); a staggering proportion no longer existed or no longer had the place of prominence they had once enjoyed.

- And then there is the question of power shifts. Changes in the law and in the distribution of information have led to the increasing power of customers, employees and shareholders. Organizations are accountable as never before and must take many different types of opinion into account. When British Gas awarded its chief executive officer (CEO) a salary package well in excess of £1 million while at the same time cutting the pay of some showroom staff, it found that it was unable to avoid the power of public indignation; an indignation that (at the time of writing) is being sharpened into retributive taxes!

And then these implications can be further refined as concrete *issues* for business. These are many and varied but some of the inescapable ones could be summarized as the following necessities:

- a need to focus on the right market;
- a need to obtain critical mass within the market;
- a need to get the people side right;
- a need to get the shape of the organization right.

These issues may sound simple, may sound obvious but none of them are. In fact they represent a whole host of challenges and a myriad of questions to be asked.

## The right market

A whole range of questions exist here. Markets change, customer preferences alter and the technology changes the face of products all the time. Consequently, a number of questions have to be asked. Who is now my competitor? What is uniquely competitive about my product? Where should I pitch my product – as cheap and cheerful or at the quality end of the market? What can I do that will make people seek my product out before all others? What value will my exertions return to shareholders and how will they react?

## Obtaining critical mass

Critical mass can be defined as growing large enough to influence what happens in your environment simply by being there; after that you can dictate terms, affect prices and control entry to it. Organizations seek to obtain it through the acquisition of other organizations, merging and sometimes by inviting others to take them over. Other methods of achieving quick growth can be through joint ventures, strategic alliances and consortia; however, critical mass is not simply a matter of size – being big, if you do not keep up-to-date with technological and other changes, is not enough in itself, as IBM found out to its cost!

A far better means of obtaining critical mass is through adopting an *inclusive* attitude as recommended by the RSA Inquiry (1995) into 'Tomorrow's Company'. In the report, the attitudes in tomorrow's company are summarized as adopting an inclusive approach to business leadership, society and people, meaning that: 'Tomorrow's company values reciprocal relationships. It thinks win–win, understands that by focusing on all those who can contribute to the business it should improve returns to stakeholders ... Yesterday's companies are locked in adversarial relationships ... tomorrow's company is managed by people who can hold collaboration and competition in their heads at the same time ... yesterday's companies are managed by people who see only themselves and their immediate colleagues as us, and everybody else as them'. This of course is a far more open and creative approach and one more likely to foster creative solutions to problems; we will explore it further in Chapter 5.

## The people side

There are a number of powerful forces at work in the people side of business. Most of them are not the result of legislation, and are all the more powerful for it. The hacking out of layers within organizations has resulted in increased teamworking and the need for different leadership styles. At the same time, people are demanding more of their organizations in terms of investment in their own growth and development while they are employed and enjoying new, flexible working practices. At the same time, however, there is no longer an expectation that the organization will provide them with a job for life but rather that, by working for it, it will enhance their overall employability either as full-time employees with other organizations or as self-employed contractors. The nature of the 'employment deal' has changed – neither side can continue to rely on old certainties. Motivation and reward are still key concepts but it would be naïve to assume that they mean the same as a few years ago.

## The shape of the organization

Here again, a number of issues are having to be faced. With key emphasis on flexibility and adaptability, with pundits now talking about the agile company or the fast organization, there is a pressing need for businesses to rethink their shape, their structures and the very way in which they do business. How many layers of management are practical? How should they operate within new structures and systems? Structures which have often dispensed with conventional divisions between departments through the creation of cross-functional teams? What are the implications for both disseminating and understanding information within these new structures?

Taken as a whole, the complex cocktail of issues and factors described above leads to one conclusion...

**Being strategic – not an option**

All of the above could be summarized as illustrating the pressing need for people to anticipate, be aware of and above all to take appropriate action in the light of the changes and issues that affect the business, social and economic environments – the environments that affect the lives of us all. In other words they emphasize the pressing need for people in all occupations and at all levels in organizations to be strategic!

A powerful example of this requirement can be found in The British Quality of Management Awards, sponsored by MORI and PA Sundridge Park. For several years they have been analysing those factors within organizations that have been seen to make a major contribution to delivering sustainable growth in shareholder value (or citizen value in the public sector). They created a list of criteria based on observation of successful companies over a long period and then asked a number of people the following question:

> Think about the quality of management in terms of future development of a company. These are all attributes of senior level management which might contribute to how well a company develops. Which four or five of them do you consider most relevant for such development?

Respondents, who were sub-divided into those from the City, business and finance and then captains of industry, were then given a list of 20 attributes. Each time the Quality of Management Awards have been run, respondents have placed two categories head and shoulders above all others – strategy and leadership (see Figure 1.1). If we assume that it is leaders at all levels within businesses who must be generating or implementing the strategies, then the whole focus of the report emphasizes one requirement above all others – the need for *strategic leadership*, the need for people with responsibility to think and act strategically. But first it is necessary for them to fully understand the meaning of the term strategy and to appreciate what 'being strategic' means for them.

So, if we can accept that being strategic is not an option but an absolute necessity, then it is time to define strategy in a way that makes it a useful and purposeful tool for us all.

## Further definitions

Many organizations are now sharing their overall strategies with their staff. In order to make this process successful it is necessary for them first to define what they themselves mean by strategy. This in itself is a useful process and has often helped to further clarify the term. One such definition was made by the Compass Group plc, leaders in industrial catering and arguably one of the world's fastest-growing service companies. The definition it has released to its managers on a global basis reads as follows:

> Strategy is the formulation and execution of an integrated set of actions based on customer needs, which identify both the essential positioning ('Where to compete') and the competitive advantages ('How to compete') necessary to create value superior to competition and thereby meeting our financial goals.

Compass goes on to elaborate on the where and how (which of course is confidential to them) and it is this elaboration that turns their definition of strategy into something that drives their business forward. The Compass definition is useful – it poses a couple of key questions:

- How do we compete?
- Where do we compete?

And these questions will inevitably shape future plans and policies. However, as a definition it is very specific to one organization's needs at a particular moment in its development; perhaps we should look at a more general definition. One such definition was made by Ram Gharan, academic, consultant and ex-member of the Harvard faculty, who made the following statement:

> Strategy is shaping and reshaping a 'central idea' or 'prevailing paradigm' in detail and implementing it persistently and consistently.

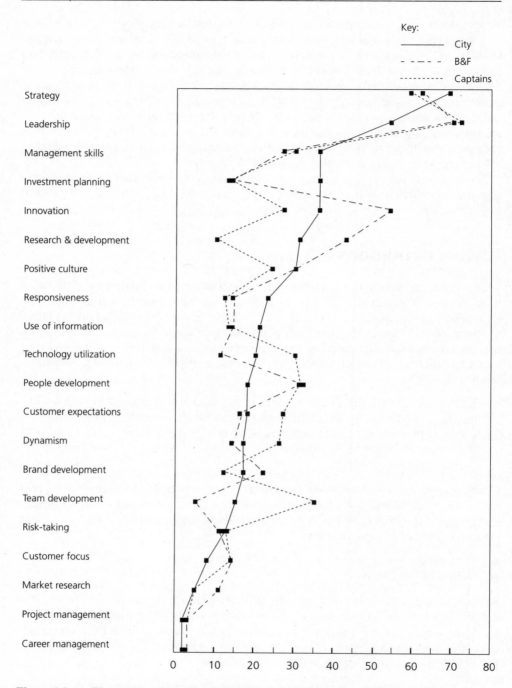

**Figure 1.1    The quality of management – how they voted (*Source:* MORI and PA Consulting Group)**

You may think that this definition takes us neatly from the over-specific to the obscure. What can he be talking about? How can this statement be used as a basis for action in business; or anywhere else for that matter? The fact is that, obscure though this definition may be, it is a good one and dovetails in well with the demands of the ever-changing global and business environments. What we must now do is 'de-jargonize' it, add to it and restate it in a way that makes it a usable tool. Before doing so, however, it is useful to look at one other attempt to define the components of success in modern business and organizational life.

In their best-selling book *The Discipline of Market Leaders* (1995), Michael Treacy and Fred Wiersema stated that there were three value disciplines for success – *operational excellence, product leadership and customer intimacy* – a statement that is not a million miles away from that made by the Compass Group. But they then went on to define exactly what they meant in far more detail. They stressed that simply to 're-engineer a company's business process is not enough, it's not by any means all that a company needs'. If a company was to achieve and sustain (market) dominance, it must first decide where it will stake its claim in the market-place and what kind of value it will offer its customers – then it would be in a position to identify its core competencies and re-engineer its processes. Crucially, they stated that the 'choice of value discipline must be made'. But what does this then mean?

The authors go on to clarify this statement by saying that value has come to mean three different things: having the best products; having the best total solution to customers' needs, and delivering it at the best total cost. They state quite categorically that market leaders must choose to excel in delivering extraordinary levels of one particular value. The very act of *choosing* a discipline is the first choice of winners! Later on, in talking about why companies deliver superior value, they state that companies can seize certain advantages through *focus*, for example ensuring at all times that your service levels are excellent and seen by customers as 'hassle free'.

Two key words have emerged to augment the definition made by Ram Gharan – *choice* and *focus*. Now it is time to move on to the definition of strategy that we will use as the central theme of this book!

Brian Pitman, chairman of Lloyds Bank, defined strategy as:

### Focus and hard choices

This is a useful definition as it implies that becoming strategic is not necessarily an easy process. It also reflects the key talents hinted at so far. The definition can be refined, however, to make it more action-based as strategy above all else is about action. The final definition, therefore, reflects this requirement for action and puts the word strategy into the overall business and social environment in which we all work and live:

> Strategy is the process of adopting a new mindset, of surveying the overall situation, of focusing on a goal and making the hard choices necessary to achieve it.

But what does this mean for you?

One of the main problems that face both individuals and organizations is that most people do not regard themselves as either capable of being strategic or of there being any requirement for them to be so. The 'I'm just an employee . . .' mind-set prevails and this frustrates many a career and many an organization. One thing must be made clear: for those who wish to succeed, strategic thinking must start early in their careers and, if this does happen, then both employee and organization will benefit. As Porter said, 'Strategy is not just for top managers.' But this in itself implies a great deal and implies a journey of discovery for the new strategist – a journey that has no end but which will take the new strategist through three stages of development: birth, growth and maturation. But then maturation in itself is a dangerous phase as it implies a lapse of many of the attitudes and energies that make for good strategic thought and action in the first place. So, perhaps we should refer to a process of birth, growth, brief maturation followed by rebirth – strategists should be phoenix-like in constantly reinventing their thinking processes as well as their approaches to action.

So in coming back to what the definition means to you, it is necessary to give a warning: creating and implementing strategies requires you to abandon many old thinking patterns as well as old approaches to work. It requires an acceptance of the phoenix-like approach – just when you think that you have got there and that a number of certainties have been reached, you will be required to challenge both the certainties as well as the methods you used to reach them – and, in all probability, start all over again.

If this appears unreasonable, then look back to the brief synopsis of the business and world environment earlier in this chapter. You may have found it gloomy and threatening, you may have felt that it posed many more questions than it attempted to answer. This was deliberate; it is certainly not the purpose of this book even to try to answer the huge questions that face this planet; however, in alluding to them, hopefully the absolute need for people to have flexible, strategic mindsets has been illustrated. An open, questioning attitude is always the first step in examining and conquering complexity. If you examine total chaos, for example in the form of a huge set of randomly generated numbers that appear to have no pattern, structure or meaning, and continue to study it for long enough, then patterns of repeating sequences will start to emerge within the chaos. These patterns, called fractiles, will then repeat themselves and can be portrayed through computer-generated images as beautiful but ever-repeating patterns. 'So what?' you might say.

Well, study and the gleaning of the first elements of knowledge can lead on to great things. In the Second World War, British mathematicians studied and finally broke the Nazi Enigma code – a supposedly unbreakable code which U-boat commanders used to communicate with their high command. The first breakthrough came via the realization that the code had one inherent piece of logic – a letter could never be represented by itself in the code (that is, an A could never be an A and a B could never be a B, etc.); after that patterns began to emerge and the code was eventually cracked, a vital step in winning the Battle of the Atlantic.

But first, a few final definitions. There is a difference between strategic thinking, formulation of strategy and other subsets of the overall 'management' of an organization. Categories within these subsets include *planning* and *action*. Planning could be defined as the more detailed scheduling of action within the overall strategy itself while action is the equivalent of military tactics, the final combination of task, plan and activity that delivers the final result. While we will look at planning and action later in this book as they are the mechanisms by which results are delivered, the main focus will be on the essential core skills of strategic thinking and strategy formulation – skills that hopefully can benefit you in any path of business or life itself.

## The way ahead

The first steps in this book, consequently, will be to take you on a journey through what being strategic actually involves; it will challenge your thought processes and invite you to break them down into their component parts, look at them, throw out the old or obsolete and adopt the new. In doing so, it will examine where your thinking patterns come from and give you a model to help focus on what is already strategic within yourself, where your main source of creativity lies and then what talents can be used to implement the strategies that have been created.

Subsequently, we will focus in on a number of strategic models, which will give you a menu of tools from which to pick the best method of strategic analysis to meet your need. We will then move on to examine the core skills needed to manage change, sow the seeds of innovation and overcome the difficulties inherent in implementing strategies. The approach will be pragmatic in so far as at the end of each chapter a number of points will be set out for you to consider and hopefully to use as a basis for action.

But if most journeys start with packing, the assembly of what is required, this journey starts with unpacking!

## Action points for consideration

● Examine the various definitions of strategy. To what extent are they applicable in your job or life? If they are not, then why not?

● Analyse in which areas of your business and personal lives it would be useful to have long-term plans based on well-thought-out perspectives.

● Look at the current business, social and political scenarios as portrayed in the press and media. What patterns can be identified and what effect might they have on your business in both the long and short term? How might what you see influence your thoughts and actions?

● Consider whether the markets for your business's products or services are changing. Once again, what actions are implied?

● With the Quality of Management Awards in mind, think about your job and the degree to which it incorporates elements of strategy, leadership and management. Notwithstanding your level of seniority, is there a correct balance for you to choose in order to be effective?

# Chapter 2

# Thinking and acting strategically

Strategy, the achievement of focus and the making of hard choices, enables you to change and affect your external world. But the overall process starts from within.

If you want to act strategically start by examining your own thinking, your patterns of thought, your approaches – the possibilities of new ways of thinking that may be open to you as strategies are in themselves far more than just plans, they are about identifying the possibilities of any situation as well as eventually setting the direction towards a goal. While the process of identifying and reaching the goal may be compared to that of preparing for and embarking on a long walk – you must be fit for it and have the right equipment – by the same token, to be fully strategic you must have developed your mental muscles, have examined your mental kit bag and repacked it if necessary in order to be best able to conceive strategies that take the organization in the right direction before starting to implement them.

So the first step in either thinking or acting strategically is that of pausing, taking stock; of self-knowledge, of allowing the possibilities to present themselves to you through a process of applied reflection and consideration of the options rather than of rushing into hurried decision-making and frantic action – this is what could be termed rhino management. The rhino is a noble beast with several notable characteristics; it is very short-sighted and has a tendency to charge without warning if it thinks it sees a potential enemy, accelerating its considerable bulk to some 30 miles per hour very rapidly. So, for example, it may dimly perceive a TV film crew in a Land Rover a hundred yards away and, deciding that this is the enemy, charge. Unfortunately, the Land Rover moves making the rhino miss the target and run out of breath in frustration. A double frustration for in its charge it has ignored two bushes; behind one bush is an attractive rhino of the opposite sex (opportunity!), while behind the other is a hunter with a gun (threat!). Perhaps it is not for nothing that the poor rhino is a threatened species.

So the successful strategists will be anything but rhino-like; this does not mean that they will not be purposeful or swift to act when the time comes, but it does mean that they will take time to assess both themselves and the situation requiring decisions before charging ... I mean embarking on a series of purposeful, measured actions.

In this chapter we will look at ways of examining the mental toolkit necessary to embark on the journey towards strategic thinking, the path towards selecting the most creative approaches and then in turn apply these criteria in defining a powerful model for strategic action.

## Examining your thinking

There is a wise old expression: 'If you always do what you've always done, you'll always get what you've always got.' This sentiment applies equally to thought as it does to action. Static thinking produces static results if it brings any results at all – the main problem for many people is that they do not recognize when they are the victims of static thinking. Our mindsets, the overall way in which we view the world, are often called paradigms and they tend to define our responses to stimuli as well as our opinions and our actions. For example, before Galileo, everybody thought that planet Earth was the centre of the universe and that all the planets orbited around it; it was not until Galileo challenged this way of thinking that anybody even conceived of any other possibility; when he asserted that the Earth was but a small planet in a vast system this 'paradigm shift' was so revolutionary in terms of redefining our relative importance in the universe that he was persecuted under the Inquisition.

Other more recent paradigm shifts have affected a number of different ways in which we live our lives. Major shifts in thinking are occurring about morals and the role of the family, for example, and in the world of work an enormous shift has occurred in the relationship between employer and employee. Until very recently, it used to be the case that individuals started out on a career with an organization on the assumption that if they worked well, 'kept their noses clean', they would have a job for life. This is now manifestly not the case; many organizations pursue open policies of easing workers in their fifties out, while others are more covert but still do the same thing – the implications for pensions, savings and the world of self-employment are immense. The resultant paradigm shift among employees has been a growth in cynicism about the motives of organizations coupled with a dramatic drop in loyalty and increasing focus on their own well-being rather than that of the organization. The harsh new world predicted by Charles Handy in *The Age of Unreason* (1988) has arrived faster than predicted.

In many societies the 40–30–30 rule now applies. Forty per cent of the working population consider themselves to have permanent tenure, 30 per cent are regarded as 'temps' and 30 per cent have very insecure tenure, have retired early or are in some way missing out on the labour market. This fact has numerous implications ranging from a low feelgood factor in the economy through to the growth of the underclass and of no-go areas as young people despair over the prospects of being able to work and to live 'conventional lives'. Perhaps an antidote to this gloomy scenario is for a paradigm shift in thinking about employment as we know it. Here are some ideas to break out of the trap:

- Scrap the retirement age – or give incentives to retain older workers.
- Give parents income to parent and assess them on the contribution they make in producing worthwhile citizens.
- Involve parents more in their children's education.
- Give organizations better incentives to retain staff as well as take on the under-privileged.
- Set up massive agencies to help those involved in any form of contract working.

These ideas may be part of a paradigm shift in the way we view both work and education that could in turn help us to avoid the gloomy scenario outlined above. Old certainties disappear and it is necessary to change one's view of the world to avoid being caught in a vacuum.

So the first step towards becoming a strategic thinker is that of examining the paradigms that govern your responses to stimuli and your subsequent actions. In considering your paradigms, please note that it is not a question of reconsidering your fundamental values; these can remain but you must be aware of the changes happening elsewhere (for example, I deplore the breakdown of the traditional family and its threat by other values. I must accept, however, that thoughts about family and parenthood have shifted and will probably continue to shift; I cannot make assumptions based on what I would like to see happening!) Here is a question to consider:

> What are my prevailing paradigms about work and society – do they really reflect what is going on out there? If not, do I need to reflect on my mindset in order to make me more responsive to current and future challenges?

The first step in developing your ability as a strategic thinker is that of being aware of your prevailing paradigms and of accepting that they must be put aside in order to open your mind to future possibilities. For example, many old paradigms about how business should be conducted are being challenged by the concept of the 'agile company'. Before we examine this concept, however, it may be useful to take a look at Henry Mintzberg's (1996) paradigm-bending attempt to shake people out of their complacency about what made for good management. Management can get in the way of success, he stated and put forward the following musings, apologizing to anybody that he had not offended in the process!

- Organizations don't have tops or bottoms.
- It's time to delayer the delayerers.
- Lean *is* mean and doesn't even improve long-term profits.
- The trouble with most strategies is chief executives who believe themselves to be strategists.
- Decentralization centralizes, empowerment disempowers and measurement doesn't measure up.
- Great organizations once created don't need leaders.
- Great organizations have souls; any word with a 'de' or a 're' in front of it is likely to destroy these souls.

- It is time to close down conventional MBA programmes.
- Organisations need continuous care, not interventionist cure.

You may or may not agree with these challenges. Nevertheless, they are successful in that they jerk people out of their complacency about what makes for success. As someone who works in and with organizations I strongly agree with some of Mintzberg's paradigm-busters – take for example his statement 'measurement doesn't measure up'; a direct challenge to the old maxim 'If you can't measure it, you can't manage it!' As someone who has experienced the stultifying effects of burgeoning bureaucracy, the growth of numerical controls masquerading under the name of empowerment with its frantic attempts to measure volume and quantity rather than value added, I would add another statement to the list:

- You cannot measure common sense; attempting to do so produces the opposite!

It is now time to look at the reason *why* it is so necessary to challenge our paradigms.

## Companies in the twenty-first century – the agile company

The PA Consulting Group has conducted a survey of organizations in 20 countries, seeking to understand just how agile organizations are across the world, how demanding their markets are and what they were doing to become more agile. It has found that the agile company will be one that is:

- Obsessed with providing customer value – prepared to put in significant effort to establish exactly what it is that their customers want, and then putting those things first.
- Dynamically networked – the organization needs to be at the centre of a number of interacting networks to enable it to gather knowledge and use expertise quickly and as well as possible.
- Rigorously focused on creating value through knowledge – the organization will be learning and focused on new learning at all times.
- Continuously adaptive, able to change its way of working in order to deliver optimum value to customers and to do so at a moment's notice.
- Ruthlessly decisive – must be prepared to dispose of parts of itself that do not contribute to the goal of providing optimum value.

The survey draws an analogy with a Formula One racing team in that, in the business environment, like the race track, competition and technology are both moving increasingly fast. Agility means combining all the desired qualities within a unified strategic approach, one that is based upon a candid review of the prevailing paradigms within the organization.

# Busting your personal paradigms

Paradigms have been defined, what they are and why we need to challenge them. But how do you do so? What are the keys to creative, innovative approaches? Where do you start?

The answer lies in the type of open-ended questions just put forward. There is a fundamental difference between a closed question that is specific and often demands just a 'yes' or 'no' answer in response and an open question that both challenges the other person's thinking as well as giving them far more scope in the way that they reply. For example, there is a world of difference between 'Should we move into the micro-electronics market?' as a question and 'What markets should we be moving into?' as a similar but in fact totally different question.

Rudyard Kipling summarized the power of the open question by talking about the usefulness of simple words such as 'What?', 'Why?', 'When?', 'How?', 'Where?' and 'Who?' He aptly concluded that the effectiveness of those words in helping him form short but searching questions had taught him everything he knew, and he praised these words as being 'six honest serving men'. It is through using these simple words that we can challenge our paradigms, reconstitute them where necessary and take a step towards truly creative thinking. They can be used to launch challenging questions that open up our thinking about a situation and nudge us into a strategic perspective. For example:

- What markets should we be in?
- What approaches might work for us in the future?
- What would be the consequences of this approach?

- Why are we doing it this way?
- Why have our markets always responded like this?
- Why don't we do things differently?

- When should we start?
- When was the last time anybody tried this?
- When will we know we have been successful?

- How should we organize ourselves?
- How would our staff react?
- How would our competitors react to this initiative?

- Where should we be positioning ourselves?
- Where are the best opportunities for growth?
- Where have others failed?

- Who has tried this before?
- Who could help us in our venture?
- Who in fact are our real competitors?

These are all strategic questions; individually they are all powerful but when you mix them up they take on extra strength and can challenge, break down, open up and rebuild – they are the keys to innovation, insight and creativity.

At PA Sundridge Park we often start programmes by challenging groups of delegates to think more creatively and to use the teams we place them in as a vehicle for more effective learning. We start the process by giving them a number of brain teasers or lateral thinking questions to solve in their groups via the use of open-ended questions. Here is one of the questions we have used:

> A man is pushing his car and stops opposite a hotel. Suddenly he realizes he is bankrupt. Why?

The rhino approach will be to jump in with a number of guesses. 'Well, he owned the hotel and sees the bailiffs outside it!' 'There is a petrol station beside the hotel and his credit card bounces', etc., etc. All wrong!

The key is to bombard the subject with open-ended questions. Why is he pushing the car in the first place? What sort of road is it? What is so special about being outside the hotel? Why should arrival outside the hotel signify bankruptcy? What makes his car easy to push?

Persistent questioning of this nature usually enables the team to make the paradigm shift. Suddenly there is illumination – if we question the very nature of the road and the car, if we think of different ways of pushing a car, then the penny drops … the man is playing Monopoly and he has landed on a square in which an opponent has built a hotel, thereby enabling him to charge high rent!

And the successful busting of paradigms moves us swiftly into the realms of creative thinking – the mental space where strategies are conceived and developed.

## Creating your own creativity

A very basic process for moving towards strategic action runs as follows:

1. Examine your scenario
2. Identify the forces for change
3. Examine the prevailing paradigm within your business/situation
4. Think creatively to develop new approaches/goals
5. Determine the new goals
6. Decide on the actions to reach them.

As a process this requires considerable elaboration to make it a useful tool and it will be developed at the end of this chapter as well as in Chapter 3. It does, however, illustrate the place of creativity in both strategic thinking and action; so we now need to further examine the concept as well as how to develop it.

Ned Herrmann (1996), the originator of the concept of brain dominance, has come up with one of the best definitions of creativity. It is, he states, 'An ability to challenge assumptions, recognize patterns, see in new ways, make connections, take risks and seize upon a chance'. To this definition I would simply add the following – 'and in doing so make something new or tangibly different that is of substantial value'.

So how do we achieve this? To start with, it is necessary to want to be creative, to accept that there are different sorts of creativity as well as different sorts of imagination – the place where most creativity is born. But the beginning is the *will*, just as the will, or purpose, is the initiator of the strategy. George Bernard Shaw seemed to understand the process as he made an insightful, if unwitting, link between creativity and strategy. 'Imagination is the beginning of creation. We imagine what we desire; we will what we imagine; and at last we create what we will.'

From the will must then flow a number of practices and processes which will exercise the mind and develop its creativity. Some of these processes are deliberate and can be practised as team exercises while others are subconscious and simply need your time as well as your conscious permission for them to take place. As creative individuals make better creative team members, let us start with the growth of individual creativity.

There are a number of stages in the growth of personal creativity and many have studied them, from David Campbell at The Center for Creative Leadership to Ned Herrmann. With slight differences most people agree that, with the exception of a few flashes of brilliance, most creativity comes as the result of a definable process which follows these lines.

*Desire*
This is being aware of a problem or of a need for change or simply of the wish to create something new, whether it is to do with business or is something artistic. Few positive developments have emerged either from apathy or from decadence. Desire for beauty, for novelty, or to build is the starting point.

*Engagement*
This is confronting the problem with the desire, mulling it over, jotting down thoughts, weighing up the odds, the first session at the PC or the drawing board, consciously trying to free the mind of the fetters of the old. Searching out and confronting any paradigms that may be holding you back, doing battle with them. There is a wise saying, 'Old habits are like light chains; seldom noticed until you try to break them.'

*Incubation*
This is usually the unconscious stage of the process. The mind will tackle a problem, confront it and worry at it like a dog with a bone, usually while you are asleep or deeply relaxed. This is a vital stage and neglected at your peril. Not for nothing is there the expression 'to sleep on it'. So give yourself time to be creative, make it a relaxing and enjoyable experience.

*Illumination*
This is the stage where the new idea or the insight hits you, sometimes right between the eyes. Illumination cannot be forced; you cannot say to yourself, 'It is

now time for me to have the great idea or insight'; it will come in its own good time, often when you least expect it. One of my colleagues used to hope for good ideas to come to him when jogging and, as he normally ran the same route, would challenge himself to have had an idea or have solved a problem by the time he passed a certain tree; after which he would agree with himself to stop trying. Paradoxically, most of his best thoughts would come to him after he had passed the tree and had stopped trying to force the pace.

### Testing

Is the idea any good? Is it possible to select and home in on one of the range of possibilities that may have presented themselves at the illumination stage? Does it stand up to analysis? Where and how can we use it? This final evaluative stage is a vital one as it forces the idea to pass the 'so what?' test and leads on to the final stage.

### Application

Putting it into action. What happens next? The indispensable stage for strategists or creative artists alike. An action without thought is not very much, but a thought without action is nothing at all!

The creative process is very similar to the overall model of strategic development we shall illustrate and use later in this chapter. This may be pure coincidence; I prefer to think of it as the product of unseen but inescapable logic and truth. The law governing the formation of fractiles may be at work again! So how do we get the overall process moving either individually or in groups?

## A metaphor for creativity – jazz in the workplace

Creativity can be developed either individually or in teams. With the individual, the process usually follows the preceding lines. However, in the case of groups or teams it is often different. Much has been written on the subject of brainstorming and the power of the team and it is not the intention to go through the list of approaches such as Six Hat Thinking or Pin Point which have been designed to maximize the creativity of a group of people; these techniques can be found by reading the works of Edward de Bono and others. Indeed, it is quite possible for a group to become stultified if it follows a technique too pedantically or self-consciously – the approach can impose its own limitations. Instead, it is more profitable to look at the overall forces and influences that help a group to generate creative ideas. Here the metaphor is that of the jazz group and this is a theme that has already been developed by a number of people, most notably Stan Gryskiewicz (1992) at the Center for Creative Leadership in North Carolina and John Kao (1996) in *Jamming: The Art and Discipline of Business Creativity*.

Arguably jazz musicians are both more creative and better technicians than their classical counterparts; they start from a single idea, pull it apart, build on it, test it to its limits, turn it upside down, inside out, seek out the essential energy within it, allow different members of the combo to individualize it and show personal brilliance before fusing all efforts together into a harmony or product that is creative, satisfying yet challenging. The classical musician has in the meanwhile followed the rules laid down by the original creative genius and usually has had much of his or her spontaneity drilled out in the pursuit of 'technique'. If this paragraph has irritated some readers, that is fine – it has been a deliberate attempt to rattle some cages and perhaps to shift a paradigm or two!

To reach this creative environment, a number of preconditions are necessary in the environment. Jazz or jamming needs a mixture of free expression and discipline; it needs an environment where mistakes are tolerated in the pursuit of innovation and where testing the limits is not just encouraged but applauded by all. Look at the members of a jazz group in the full flight of improvisation; they are focused, serious but at the same time there is great joy. All are in it together and in encouraging each other to greater feats of individual expression members have the satisfaction of knowing that they are building the excellence of the final product. Whether the jamming technique used is formal brainstorming or anything else, it is the spirit, the permission to experiment given by all and to all, that is the true generator of creativity.

An example of an organization that actively encourages the creativity of its staff through the promotion of wild ideas and the use of many of the features described above is IDEO Product Development. This design firm's main product is creativity itself; creating about 90 new products per year from toothpaste containers to laptop computers. IDEO's staff work under tight time pressures but the prevailing message is that they cannot be expected to be creative without 'heavy doses of freedom and fun'. According to David M. Kelly, its founder, it is in a perpetual state of experimentation and he ardently believes that creativity is stifled when everybody has to follow the rules. Brainstorming meetings are actively encouraged and the only strict rules seem to operate around how to get the best from a brainstorm – but there is no indulgence, a key word is quickly – problems are there to be solved and beaten.

Brainstorming meetings are usually group meetings (although there is a growing tendency for virtual brainstorms via the Internet or video conferencing) but how does the individual generate creativity, or jam, alone? Anybody who has sat down alone with a guitar or at the piano will know that this is both possible and very satisfying. A number of preconditions, however, must be met to ensure the flow of creativity; they will probably differ from individual to individual but the following broad guidelines may be useful.

# Eight steps to being more creative

1.  *Want to be creative*   I believe that humans are essentially creative (just look at children) but that for many the creative urge is purged either by the educational system or by stultifying work or personal environments. Being creative is fun, it is uniquely satisfying. Allow your self to be creative; whatever creativity means to you – want it!

2. *Find your own creative space*   This can be a room, a garden, a corner with a PC, a jogging route – it is wherever you can find the space to develop your ideas or practise your art with some degree of freedom and protection from interruption. Once found, protect and develop this space – allow it to work for you.

3. *Find your own creative time*   One problem for most people is lack of time – pressures of work, of travel, of relationships, press in and restrict the opportunity for self-expression and creativity. Paradoxically, for many, the time comes once they have retired and their lives have been restructured for them. However, life is not a dress rehearsal – *Carpe Diem!* Seize the day! Find that time!

4. *Visualize what success will look like*   What is it you want to achieve, to produce, to build or what problems do you want to solve? Try to imagine what it will be like, look like and feel like when you have achieved your goal. At times creative people may appear unfocused; that is simply because you may be observing them in mid-process – behind it lies strong determination driven by great focus.

5. *Clear your mind*   A mind cluttered by minutiae, by day-to-day issues and problems will not be creative. A friend of mine has an expression 'Administrivia'; he hates it but accepts that it is a necessary part of work and life. We all have administrivia to get through, but we need to put it out of the way to allow the imagination to flourish.

6. *Exercise your imagination*   Astronauts are taught to daydream as a means of preserving sanity during long trips in space. Daydreaming can unlock many doors as well as take us back to a child-like state where our minds are not cluttered by assumptions and preconceptions. We might like to imagine what our businesses would look like to a child – what would they approve of, what would they question, what would they find ridiculous? A powerful example of this can be seen in the fantasy film *Big* where a boy and a man swap bodies. The boy has to go to work and through asking genuinely naïve questions is soon hailed as a genius and promoted!

7. *Freewheel and rein in*   Follow the jamming process; having explored all possibilities, focus back onto the product. What tangible output do you want to see? What results should be generated by solving the problem?

8. *Accept the scope and limits of your creativity*   Accept that you may be more creative in some areas than others and concentrate on those things where you can be creative. For example, if you are tone deaf, don't try to be a musician. If you can't draw to save your life don't try to be the next Degas. This applies as much to you as to attempts to evoke some sorts of creativity from those who are blatantly not suited to it. There is no point in trying to teach a pig to dance; you won't succeed and it will only annoy the pig.

   But if you feel that you can develop a skill – say that of visualizing futures for your organization or department from the basis of originally whacky ideas – then go for it!

It is on the basis of identifying different sorts of personal creativity that we can move to placing creativity into a fully strategic business context. It is my firm opinion that everybody has it in them to be creative; we are, however, all different and can be creative, or intelligent, in very different ways. It is one of the great tragedies of the human race that for too long we have been stuck with prevailing paradigms about what constitutes both intelligence and creativity. One of the great liberators in this particular field has been Ned Herrmann with his theory of brain dominance and it is this theory which we will use to make the essential link between different types of creativity and both the conception and implementation of business strategies.

## The theory of brain dominance

To become fully conversant with brain dominance, read Ned Herrmann's (1988) semi-autobiographical account of the development of the model. The synopsis given here is brief and quickly moves on to making the connection with strategic thinking. Nevertheless, a brief description of the theory's development is necessary to ensure full understanding.

Herrmann was employed by the General Electric (GE) company in the US. A physicist by training, he was also involved in HR work and had risen to a senior level within the organization. He was satisfied but did not feel fully fulfilled. He had a passing interest in the physiology of the brain and in the nature of intelligence but had not studied either in any great detail. Herrmann had been intrigued by a statement made by Professor Henry Mintzberg that it was a mystery how so many people 'could be so smart in some ways and so dumb in others', but had not taken his interest any further.

Herrmann began to suffer from a large number of blackouts which were later discovered to be due to a misdiagnosed heart condition. This prevented him from indulging in one of his major life activities, singing in public. To fill the gap, he took up painting and later sculpture, ultimately becoming a professional artist. In addition, he was happier, feeling more whole as a person than ever before. This burst of personal creativity stimulated Herrmann to discover its source and his research led him immediately to the brain. Herrmann embarked on a detailed study of the human brain and made a link between the actual physiology of the brain, the essential areas of human thought/interest and the key skills needed in business. As Head of Management Development at GE's Management Development Institute, he applied this understanding to the design and delivery of management education, including strategic planning. Herrmann also developed an instrument to measure an individual's preference for thinking in any particular way.

Based on the original and widely accepted concept of there being a split between left brain thinking and right brain thinking, that is, the left side of the brain drives logic and analysis while the right side of the brain drives emotion and intuition, Herrmann developed a metaphor for four different types of thinking, linking them loosely to the physiology of the brain but essentially asserting that the brain drives both responses to stimuli as well as activity and that we will all, to a greater or lesser extent, be governed by our preferences in response. He identified four main areas of brain activity/response, linking them to clusters of identifiable behaviours or inclinations.

## 1. The A-brain preference

This sort of thinking is dominated by a preference for logic, analysis, clarification of issues, accomplishment, mathematical calculation, technical evaluation, diagnosis, solving tough problems and intellectual clarity. This type of thinker will be challenging and can appear critical. People with a liking for this kind of thinking will be found in professions such as accountancy, engineering, science or actuarial work; they will value facts and logic above all else; often they will avoid over-indulgence in interpersonal affairs, regarding them as 'sentimental' or illogical. Herrmann gives the example of the classic A-brainer as the mythical Mr Spock from *Star Trek*: an individual totally dominated by logic who cannot understand emotion, regarding it as illogical.

## 2. The B-brain preference

Here the preference is for order, sequence and planning. 'B-brainers' are naturally conservative, like stability and structure. They are good at making plans and making sure that they are implemented in a controlled, often cautious way. Someone with a high B-brain preference will be interested in how things are to be done and will often attend to details that others will forget; they like to be in control of the way things 'roll out' and will become uncomfortable if they think that they cannot be controlled through systems or bureaucracy. An example of a B-brainer would be the classic administrator – at best they get things done, as planned and on time – on the other hand they can become inflexible, placing the roll-out of the plan above logic, reason or the human consequences of the plan.

## 3. The C-brain preference

This is the interpersonal and emotional area. The person with a high C-brain preference will relate well to other people, enjoy teamwork, tend to be emotional and be good at expressing his or her feelings, be it through talking, writing or music, and will have a strong inclination towards these activities. C-brainers will often be found as teachers, counsellors or coaches; they will be good listeners as well as good at expressing ideas. Usually they will be quick to realize the human implications of what is going on, and they are generally sympathetic and compassionate. When asked to come up with examples of classic C-brainers, people often cite agony aunts from magazines or Mother Teresa.

## 4. The D-brain preference

This is the area of vision and experimentation, of seeking the opportunities in any situation. It is the area of risk-taking, of inventing solutions, of challenging the *status quo* and of seeking out the possibilities. It is the area of new ideas, of pushing out the boundaries and of intuition. D-brained people may come across as dreamers or as overtly challenging; seldom will they come across as boring! Many famous leaders, from Hitler to Churchill, probably had well-developed D-brains, while the world of fiction (Aldous Huxley), music (Jimi Hendrix), and science (Albert Einstein) is scattered with high D-brainers. The man at Decca Records who turned down the Beatles, stating that the days of guitar-playing groups were over, was probably not D-brained!

So these are the four thinking preferences or brain dominances. They are summarized in Figure 2.1 and at this stage it is necessary to stress that we are all a mixture of all four dominances – no one can be totally dominant in one preference (unless they are Mr Spock and he was not human!). In addition, there is tension across the model, as illustrated. For example, how would Mr Spock communicate with

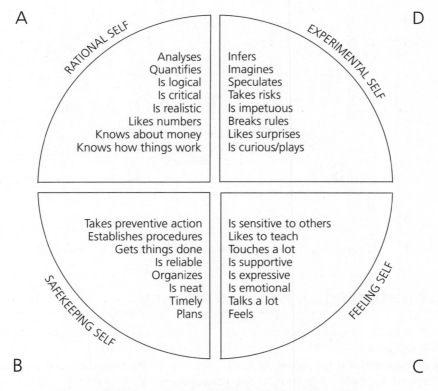

A

RATIONAL SELF

| Analyses | Infers |
| Quantifies | Imagines |
| Is logical | Speculates |
| Is critical | Takes risks |
| Is realistic | Is impetuous |
| Likes numbers | Breaks rules |
| Knows about money | Likes surprises |
| Knows how things work | Is curious/plays |

EXPERIMENTAL SELF

D

| Takes preventive action | Is sensitive to others |
| Establishes procedures | Likes to teach |
| Gets things done | Touches a lot |
| Is reliable | Is supportive |
| Organizes | Is expressive |
| Is neat | Is emotional |
| Timely | Talks a lot |
| Plans | Feels |

SAFEKEEPING SELF

FEELING SELF

B                                       C

**Figure 2.1**    **Our four different selves © 1993 Ned Herrmann Group**

Mother Teresa and how often do great visionaries see eye to eye with the bureaucrats responsible for implementing the vision? Yet all four preferences are vital both in the individual and in the organization; Ned Herrmann recognized that and plotted his model against the 'model of organizational behaviour' – we need all forms of activity as well as preferences for *doing* those activities to make for success.

Herrmann developed an instrument whereby individuals could assess their own thinking style preferences, enabling them to have diagrammatical representations of their brain dominance (see Figure 2.2), and from here it was but a short step towards charting the thinking preferences of teams and of whole organizations (see Figures 2.3 and 2.4).

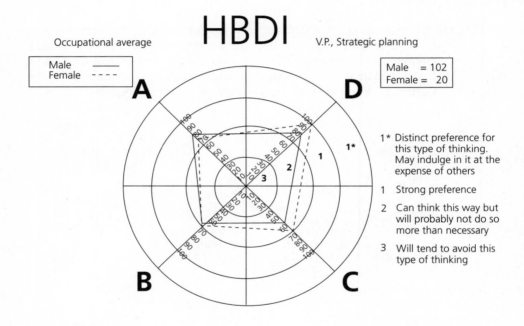

**Figure 2.2    The mapping of thinking preferences © 1993 Ned Herrmann Group**

## Linking brain dominance to strategy

So where does strategy fit into this model? In what part of our creative brains are strategies born?

The most natural home for strategic thinking is the D-brain – the area of our thinking that prods us to look at the possibilities of situations, to challenge the *status quo* and to be experimental in our approach. But being solely D-brained is

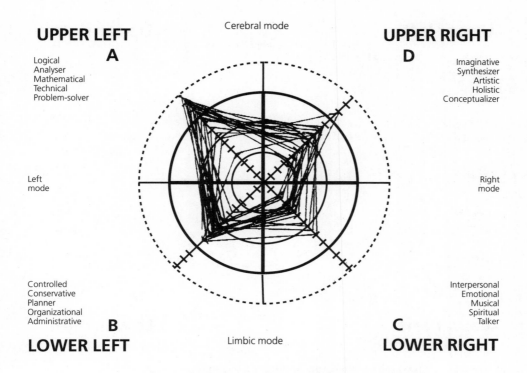

**UPPER LEFT**

**A**

Logical
Analyser
Mathematical
Technical
Problem-solver

Cerebral mode

**UPPER RIGHT**

**D**

Imaginative
Synthesizer
Artistic
Holistic
Conceptualizer

Left
mode

Right
mode

Controlled
Conservative
Planner
Organizational
Administrative

**B**

**LOWER LEFT**

Limbic mode

Interpersonal
Emotional
Musical
Spiritual
Talker

**C**

**LOWER RIGHT**

**Figure 2.3**    **Thinking preferences mapped for team members of a scientific organization**
© 1998 Ned Hermann Group

not enough to ensure that workable strategies are both conceived and implemented – we need the input of all sectors of the brain. To use a much hackneyed expression, we must be 'holistic' in approach!

In looking at the theory of brain dominance there are elements of both tragedy and triumph. The tragedy lies in the fact that for far too long educational systems have thought of intelligence primarily in terms of left-brained talents, failing to value the right brain; and the same is very often the case in organizations. It was not by accident that the example in Figure 2.4 showed a predominance in the A- and B-brains. Yet is not a high proportion of our working lives about working with and getting things done through people? And are not the implications hinted at in the agile company studies and realized in IDEO about allowing the D-brain full rein?

The triumph for us all lies in the implications arising from the theory of brain dominance, that there are many different forms of creativity and intelligence. We all have it in us to be creative in our own special ways and to make our own unique contribution to strategies using our own individual talents. True, the formulation of strategy is primarily a D-brained activity, but that does not mean to say that this mode of thinking cannot be practised, honed, polished and used. The first half of

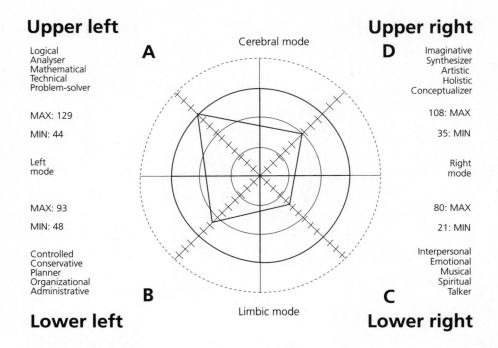

**Figure 2.4    An overall conglomerate profile for a scientific organization**
**© 1998 Ned Herrmann Group**

this chapter has been concerned with describing tools that can be used to increase your ability and willingness to use the D-brain.

However, at this stage it is necessary to introduce a new concept:

### The strategy process model

This is a five-word model of the overall process of strategy, from conception to implementation. Originally conceived by Sun Tzu in 'The Art of War', it is as valid as the day it was first used, being both simple in concept but demanding in application. Furthermore, it demands that we use both an open question approach as well as a whole-brained approach (as will be illustrated) to ensure success. The basic model goes as follows:

● Analysis
● Formulation
● Evaluation
● Implementation
● Control.

These five words represent the key stages of any strategy from inception through to its final stages. However, in order to understand the role that each stage plays we need to look at them more closely.

### Analysis

This initial stage is all about information gathering and analysis of the *status quo*. Before you can properly decide where you want to go it is necessary to know where you are at the present time. So, the strategic questions to ask at this stage would be:

- Where are we now?
- What sort of state are we in?
- Where have we come from?
- What do we look like to outsiders?

In terms of brain dominance, this is primarily an A-brain activity, involving the use of logic, statistics, diagnosis, challenge and clarification.

### Formulation

At this stage the overall strategic plan is conceived. Decisions are debated and made about the future and slowly the goal becomes clear as well as the path towards it. This is probably the most enjoyable, but at the same time the toughest, part of the process. The sort of questions that will prevail will be:

- Where do we want to get to?
- What will it be like when we have got there?
- Why do we want to do this?
- What would be the ideal state for us in the future?
- Can we be innovative here?
- What are our prevailing paradigms?
- What effect are they having?

This is the stage that calls for the most creativity, for 'out of the box' thinking, and so it is the time to exercise the D-brain. It is a time of excitement, of exploration, experimentation, seeing the end from the beginning and of allowing the possibilities of the future to dominate one's thinking.

### Evaluation

The third stage is quite different. After any brainstorm, any time of creativity, planning and innovation there is a need for objectivity, monitoring, candour and realism. This is the stage at which the formulators look at their work and ask tough questions:

- Does this make sense?
- Is this where we want to go?
- How does this stack up against other plans?
- Which of the various parts of the plan makes the most/least sense?
- What would our staff or customers think of it?

Once again we are back to the A-brain, with just a little C-brain. The creativity is analysed and challenged against the rigour of logic and hard facts – if it passes this necessary test then it is the stronger for it and any final decisions that emerge from this stage will have been honed, polished and strengthened by this baptism of fire.

### Implementation

All strategies must be turned into action and this stage involves 'planning the plan', turning it into manageable chunks, making sure that it is understood and that people both implement it and want to implement it. This stage involves both management and leadership. Key questions here will be:

- How will we get there?
- Who will we use to get there?
- What resources will be required?

This stage requires full use of the B- and C-brains. It requires the establishment of order, method, structured tasks and provisions of support mechanisms. The primary focus here is about managing the task, about achieving agreed targets on time, within budget and with people who know their roles and are motivated by them.

### Control

Once the strategic plan has been rolled out, it is, of course, vital to know whether it is getting there. This stage will involve the use of checks and measures, accounting, audit etc. but will also involve reorganization if necessary, re-motivation of people through the reiteration of the goals or vision and possibly the reworking, or re-moulding, of the plan. Key questions will be:

- Are we getting there?
- What do the numbers look like?
- How are our people reacting?
- Who should be accountable for this activity?
- Why is progress not as fast as anticipated?
- Do we need to go back to the drawing board?

If the control stage is carried out correctly it should involve all four quadrants of the brain; it requires analysis, further injections of creativity, structured tasks that help us measure and then focus on the implications for our people of what is going on.

## Conclusion

The overall process is summarized and charted in Figure 2.5. It requires creativity, leadership and management, in fact the whole range of tasks that you would find in any organization. There is some debate as to whether it is more useful to interchange stages one and two, analysis and formulation. In other words, do not become constrained in deciding where you want to get to by an analysis of where you are now. There is value in this as an alternative approach but I incline towards the classic version – your actions and the possibilities open to you *are* governed by where you are now yet knowing where you are need not prevent you from being either ambitious in desire or creative in design. However, if the brainstorm or creative thinking does not seem to be working, then try interposing stages one and two – it may be liberating!

| Action | Question |
|---|---|
| Analysis | Where are we now? |
| | Where have we come from? |
| Formulation | Why do we want to do it? |
| | Where do we want to get to? |
| Evaluation | How are we going to get there? |
| Implementation | How do we do it? |
| | Whom do we do it with? |
| Control | How do we know that we are getting there? |

**Figure 2.5    A strategic route map**

Whichever order you take the stages, the strategic planning process should exercise the paradigm busting and creative thinking discussed earlier in this chapter. It also incorporates all the elements of leadership and management needed to run a successful organization and most importantly forms the basis for the other models of strategic analysis that we shall examine in Chapter 3. However, in itself, strategic planning is a useful launch pad in achieving the focus and to point the way to the choices that must be made.

While Chapter 1 was primarily left-brain in its analysis, this chapter has attempted to be more right-brained. For the remainder of this book we will concentrate on adopting a more whole-brained approach, starting with what it means to *be* strategic. To finish on an optimistic note: recent studies indicate that creativity does not, as previously supposed, decrease with age, and so by the same token the opportunities to apply a creative approach that is blended with maturity and perspective will also increase, sowing the seeds that allow you to be truly strategic.

## Action points for consideration

● Examine where your personal main source of creativity lies. What other talents could be developed?

● Examine your own paradigms. Could they be leading you up the wrong track?

● Take time to be creative. Have you given yourself space and opportunity?

● Try out the strategy process model and ask open questions throughout.

# Chapter 3

# Being strategic

Creativity, to be effective, must be applied. Having the right attitude or mindset may be desirable in itself but unless it leads on to something worthwhile, it is of little value. You may bust your paradigms right, left and centre but, just as nature abhors a vacuum, so new ones will rush in to take their place. However, unless something changes as a result of this process, it will have been of little use. In this chapter we will make the link between thought and action. We will examine how certain elements within the strategy process model can be used to make strategies happen and will also look at some of the main models of strategic analysis in action.

Much of this chapter will be about application. It will be about moving from the original intention to be strategic through to the methods of analysis of the current situation. It will also examine the ways of generating both short- and long-term plans as well as the factors involved in making the decisions that lead to implementation of the strategies themselves. In short, we will put the strategy process model to work but first we will break it down into its component parts. We will examine a number of components both internal to the organization and external which affect a company's overall positioning in its market and then the effect that policy and philosophy may have upon that positioning.

For example, in its analysis of the global 1000 top organizations in 1997, *Business Week* (1997b) glorified in the number of American organizations heading the list and stated:

> The US keeps gaining ground in the global economy not just because many of its companies dominate the world's fastest-growing industries. Indeed, global competition has created a brand new class of blue chips. Investors no longer settle for big cap companies with steady sales and strong domestic market share. They want a worldwide brand name, super efficient production, lean management and an outspoken commitment to shareholder value.

Later it went on to comment on the slower growth of European companies stating that in some cases new socialist policies were giving job creation a higher priority than competitiveness.

None of the attributes that help the successful or the policies that slow down the less successful happen by accident; they are the result of analysis, formulation and implementation. But where do these attributes, which may flower as successful strategies or become bogged down as a result of innovation-limiting policies, come from in the first place?

# Where strategies start

A strategy is usually born out of desire. A desire to move ahead, to achieve, either personally or organizationally. We will examine how this desire is translated into leadership and action in Chapter 7. Sometimes this 'desire' is given names such as 'strategic intent' (in other words the wish and intention to conceive strategies and to act upon them) and it can be argued that this intent lies behind the birth of all strategies. But first it is necessary to look at the actual process of strategy-making, the use of methodologies and tools that turn the desire into analysis and push forward from analysis into action.

There is a wide range of strategic tools, some of which concentrate the mind primarily on analysis and which are connected with examining the health or readiness of the organization for future action. Other tools move swiftly from analysis to the stage of challenging the individual or organization to decide on a course of action.

Essentially there are three main modes or camps into which approaches to strategy-making will fall:

1.   The entrepreneurial mode
2.   The adaptive mode
3.   The planning mode.

Arguably the planning mode does not qualify fully as strategy as it concentrates to a large extent on decisions that affect the immediate future. Nevertheless, we will include it here as to talk about strategy without talking about planning – the stage that pulls together tactics and action – would leave the circle incomplete.

## *The entrepreneurial mode*

Here the approach to forming a strategy is extremely focused and the focus is upon growth and opportunity. Usually there is a central figure, a key player who is the original entrepreneur, and most of the power in the organization is usually centralized in this person. The goals of the organization will be mainly concerned with seizing the initiative, being proactive in new situations and carving out new territories. On many occasions the product will be new in itself while at other times the entrepreneur will have examined an existing situation and seized upon some angle or niche that is capable of further exploitation. The planned moves in this form of strategic planning are usually large and bold with an emphasis on flexibility. The steps must be large but they must also be nimble and capable of new movement if the demands of the situation change and growth targets become larger.

## The adaptive mode

With this mode of strategy the goals are less specific. While the entrepreneur will focus on the introduction and success of a new product, the managers within an organization that favours an adaptive mode will probably be working in a mature organization with established products and policies. The goals here will be less focused and less clear than within the entrepreneurial organization, but managers will be aware of changes to their markets and the environments in which they do business, and will react to them.

Although the goals of this organization may appear less clear, there are distinct advantages to this form of strategy-making with adaptability as the key word. The organization will be able to react to changes as they occur. The size of moves will be smaller, taking the form of a series of incremental steps, but the advantage is that those steps can change direction easily to aim at newly identified goals. Mintzberg made the analogy of the potter's wheel in describing this sort of strategy formulation. The potter has a general idea of what sort of pot to make and starts to mould the clay upon the wheel. As the pot starts to take shape, new ideas may occur or the client may express a different preference. When this happens, it is comparatively easy for the potter to take a bit off here, add a bit there – in fact to adapt the design to meet the changes in the situation which may affect the final end goal as they actually occur.

The process may appear chaotic at times but will probably give better chances of success for this type of organization than other forms of strategy-making. It also gives more opportunity to employ the techniques of strategic questioning than the entrepreneurial mode.

## The planning mode

Arguably, it is the detailed plans that turn strategies into action and, as mentioned earlier, planning can hardly be called strategy. It is, nevertheless, a crucial part of the overall process as it concentrates the strategists on the systematic and structured analysis of the way ahead while at the same time integrating the broad strategies with concrete decisions. Here, concepts such as control, ensuring predictable outcomes, efficiency of implementation and curtailment of risk are all crucial. While strategy formulation could well be termed a leadership activity, planning is clearly a management function. Paradoxically, the basic elements of successful planning are very close to the key stages of strategy and form a microcosm of the process. Nevertheless the differences are crucial, just as planning itself is crucial. Consequently, we shall examine the planning process in some detail at the end of this chapter.

# Models of strategic health analysis

Irrespective of whether you choose to use an entrepreneurial or adaptive approach to the formulation of your strategies, the overall discipline of the strategy process model (analysis–formulation–evaluation–implementation–control) will still prevail. The difference will be in 'how' the model is implemented and the first stage of analysis is often referred to as strategic health analysis. A number of methodologies have been created to assist with this part of the process and, while a scroll through them all would be exhausting for writer and reader alike, we will examine some of the most useful. In the end it is a question of choice – that of picking the method that most suits both your own preference as well as the situation in which you find yourself.

## SWOT analysis

This is one of the best known, earliest and most used models of analysis – but none the less useful for that! Like so many 'management models' it uses a four-box matrix as illustrated in Figure 3.1 and its usefulness lies in the power of the four words that form its key components:

- *S = Strengths*   All the aspects of the organization considered to be strengths are listed in this box. A strength may be anything from the quality of the management, the strength of existing products, the ability of the organization to react swiftly to changes, the investment in R&D, and so on.

- *W = Weaknesses*   In this box any aspect of an organization that could be regarded as a weakness is listed. Weaknesses may range from the control procedures to the investment in the level of training of its people and may include the age of its main product or its ability to scan new markets overseas. In short, anything that worries you about the organization may well be a weakness.

Both the strengths and weaknesses are internal to the organization and therefore this part of the analysis may come quite easily. The other two boxes may well be more challenging as they have an external focus and it is seldom as easy to analyse what is 'out there' as what may well be staring you in the face!

- *O = Opportunities*   What are the major opportunities facing the firm? What is changing out there and what's in it for you? An opportunity is anything that you can seize upon, take advantage of and plan to use or aim at with a view to achieving some form of advantage – usually financial in the form of sales or positional in terms of placing the firm so that it can move to take on further advantages. An opportunity might well be spotted in the discovery of a new technology, the failure of a competitor, the emergence of a potential new market due to deregulation, and so on.

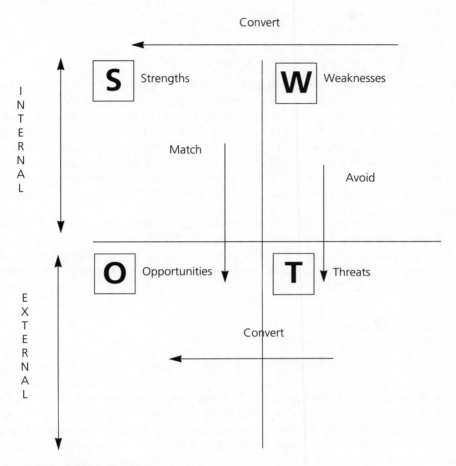

**Figure 3.1     SWOT analysis**

- *T = Threats*   These are very much what you would anticipate them to be. A competitor entering your market, the age of your staff, new technologies that may render your products obsolete, legislation that curbs your freedom to operate in what to you is the most effective way, these factors can all be classed as threats.

One of the major advantages of SWOT analysis is that it readily lends itself to the technique of brainstorming. A team can spend an enjoyable and profitable few hours analysing its organization in this way and a further benefit of the discussion is that what may appear to be a strength to one person may seem to be a weakness to another. The debate that follows can be extremely useful and can clarify many cloudy perceptions. Once the first analysis stage is complete, the team can move on to a more action-oriented form of analysis. In looking at the completed SWOT a number of questions then present themselves:

- How can our weaknesses be converted into strengths?
- How might our weaknesses be exploited by a competitor?
- Which strengths can be matched to the opportunities?
- What threats can be converted into opportunities?

If the last question may seem somewhat obscure, reflect back to the situation on the Caribbean island of Montserrat which was threatened by a volcano in 1997. This clearly was a threat to both the population and economy of this tiny island and the situation was not helped by the initial attitude of the British Government. The situation certainly looked grim – but not for all concerned! A small group of people set out to organize tourist trips to the region, cashing in on the vast pool of sightseers who had a scientific (or morbid?) interest in watching volcanic eruptions. Opportunities are often salvageable out of even the grimmest scenarios!

SWOT, like so many forms of organizational health analysis, has often been hijacked by the marketing function. Certainly, it is extremely useful in helping to plot future marketing strategies but it can most certainly be used to analyse any organization or situation so long as there is acceptance of the key underlying desire, which can be voiced by a need to:

- make better,
- take advantage of,
- improve and seize opportunities.

Finally, a different form of SWOT exists. This is known as OSWT and is a simple change around of the order of analysis. Here the opportunities are considered before all else on the basis that it is best to focus on potential opportunities before becoming trapped in an analysis of the 'here and now'. This is certainly a viable alternative approach and one worth trying at any time. A good policy would be for one group of people in an organization to work through a conventional SWOT while another tries an OSWT. Comparison of the subsequent results and recommendations would then be intriguing, possibly leading on to fruitful debate and the formulation of even better strategies.

## Core competencies

So, what is different about you? Why should we use you in preference to others? What, in particular, do you bring to the party?

These are questions that are often asked, either implicitly or explicitly, when one firm sets out to do business with another. Often the invitation to tender documents that are sent out before new business is agreed on challenge those replying to answer questions such as these; it is an arrogant or insensitive bidder that does not at least anticipate them when tendering for the business in question. If this appears to apply mainly to business-to-business marketing, then think again. When it comes to retail selling, the shopper continually looks for something unique, something special, in the product that he or she buys. We are continually bombarded with statements such as 'Only at X can you get...' – something special is being offered. Other slogans hint that you will have some unique upper hand if you buy their products or do business with them – 'If anyone can, Canon can.' At its most extreme the gullible shopper is made to pay to become a walking advertisement for the product. Simply to be seen wearing the Nike, Adidas or Gucci logo is 'cool' and the predominant logo often obviates the need for any further design!

So what is behind it all? Hamel and Prahalad (1990) stated in the *Harvard Business Review* that 'You can miss the strength of competitors by looking at their end products, in the same way you miss the strength of a tree if you look only at its leaves.' They went on to say that although a company does rely on selling its goods and services at sufficient volumes to create healthy profits, in the long run its competitiveness comes from its ability to build and develop the core competencies that lead on to new products or in some way give that extra edge. But what exactly is a core competency?

In answering that question, we return to the concept of 'that extra edge' – the differentiator. Core competencies are the result of the collective efforts and learning of the organization. The way that it has learnt to co-ordinate the different skills that go into the making up of its products and to take advantage of the possibilities arising from its technological processes. For something in an organization to be regarded as a core competency there are three tests that must be satisfied:

1.   The competency must provide access to a wide variety of markets.
2.   It must, in the client's perception, deliver real, visible and substantial benefits.
3.   It is difficult or preferably impossible to imitate.

Almost since the beginning of time organizations have been subconsciously analysing their core competencies when formulating their strategies. What Hamel and Prahalad (1990) have done in defining them more clearly has been to turn them into targets. A key question now must be, 'Do we have any core competencies? If not, what must we do, what must we learn, in order to develop them?'

And, of course, it is not easy. Virgin Atlantic may have thought that they had a core competency when they introduced the idea of chauffeur-driven cars to take business class travellers to the airport – for a while they held an advantage, but it was just too easy to imitate! Harder to imitate are technological competencies such as laser technology, fibre optics and precision engineering. Whatever field you are in, a key question to ask must be, 'What can I uniquely bring to the world that will enable me more easily to sell my product or services?' Once identified, it is a wise move to tell the marketplace what you have to offer – in doing so, you are in fact making a clear marketing statement and one that will quickly be read by competitors as part of a benchmarking exercise.

## Benchmarking

Closely allied to the concept of core competencies as a tool of strategic health analysis is that of benchmarking. Here the concept is relatively simple. An organization will look across to other organizations which may or may not be direct competitors, but which are known to be supremely good at some aspect of business, in order to see what it is they excel at. Once you have identified those things that make a particular organization excellent in a particular area, the challenge is to see whether it can be replicated in your own business. The benchmark then is the supreme standard that a firm must set out to attain, and the areas for which it sets out to obtain benchmarks, as well as the ways it plans to attain the standards, will be determinants of its future strategy. Examples of capabilities that a firm may wish to benchmark against could be:

- Speed of delivery
- Links between market research and production
- After-sales service
- Communication to employees
- Complaint handling
- Technical excellence.

As a management tool, benchmarking has been around for many years and stems from the fact that in 1979, Xerox, the originators of the discipline, found that the retail price of Canon photocopiers was less than Xerox's manufacturing costs. Time for a rethink! Most organizations would now say that they do some form or other of benchmarking.

In fact, there are very few areas of business that cannot be benchmarked and in looking across to another organization the key question must be, 'What is it that they do that makes them so good in this respect? How are they organized to make them so effective? What will we need to do, or change, to put us in this league?' In many cases the organization you are benchmarking will not be a direct competitor and so a direct request for information may give you what you want. If the organization is a competitor, you may need to speak to mutual customers in order to establish exactly why they are so good. Performance improvement is at the core of benchmarking; it identifies and measures the gap, helps to set strategies and plans for improvement, and then by stimulating a curiosity can provide the stimulus to close that gap.

As a tool for analysis, benchmarking has been growing in popularity over the last few years. It is useful in so far that it promotes best practice but dangerous when it makes people copy others slavishly without looking to see how they themselves can be innovative. Use, but handle with care!

## Porter's five forces model

Michael Porter has become one of the most respected gurus in the field of business strategy and it certainly is not possible or appropriate to do more than summarize his model here as it is the subject of a long book and many subsequent articles and commentaries.

Briefly, Porter asserts that there are five forces that govern the profitability of any industry and that these forces are interrelated and impact upon each other. In talking about an industry's profitability, Porter is also making clear statements about the determinants of an organization's success. His model, summarized in Figure 3.2, is detailed, complex and forces you as a strategist to think across a wide range of the features of your business as well as the larger market and industry context in which it operates. As can be seen, all the determinants need to be considered and are valid. However, the order in which they are described below is not, in itself, significant.

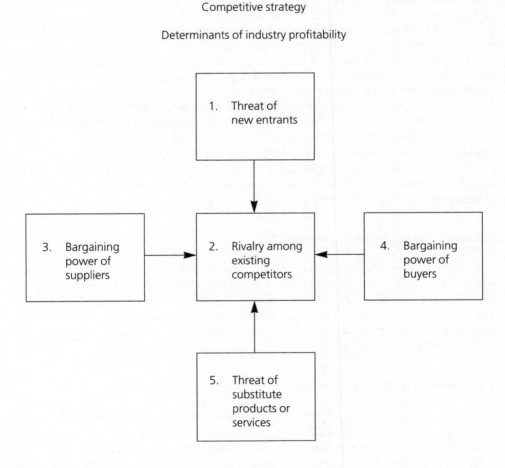

Competitive strategy

Determinants of industry profitability

**Figure 3.2** **Porter's five forces model**

## 1. Threat of new entrants

If you are trying to enter a new marketplace or trying to protect your position within it a number of factors need to be considered. Among them are economies of scale; for example, existing firms may be better established and able to produce their products at lower cost. How can you as a new entrant compete with the advantages of a competitor's economies of scale? How can your organization achieve them for itself?

Then there is the advantage of brand identity. It gives a huge advantage if your organization is an international name such as Coca-Cola or Marks and Spencer. Alternatively, if your product has become the generic name for the class of goods in which it sits, such as Hoover for vacuum cleaners or Coke for soft drinks of a particular sort. The advertising costs of competing with a well-established brand are enough to prevent many potentially good new products entering a market, as are the capital requirements – the costs of borrowing money or of setting up new plant, buying in expertise and setting up an organization.

Other entry barriers can be summarized as the barriers of learning – established firms will have a great deal more knowledge, for example access to distribution; you will need to set up distribution channels for your product and competitors can make life very difficult here (hence the huge rise of direct marketing). In addition the new entrant may face barriers in the form of government policy, rules and regulations. But in the end, the most potent barrier is that of retaliation from within the market – an established organization can lower its prices in such a way as to make profits impossible for a new entrant, or in some cases revert to the 'dirty tricks department' as Richard Branson alleged was the case when Virgin Atlantic started to compete with British Airways.

## 2. Rivalry among existing competitors

A variety of facts will determine the nature and extremity of rival organizations within an industry. Among others, they can be summarized as the overall rate of growth in the industry – after all, if the cake is growing there will be more chance of everyone getting a sizeable slice – the diversity of competitors – the extent to which buyers can, or will, wish to choose between them – and the dangers of there being over-capacity which may well force price wars.

## 3. Bargaining power of suppliers

Those who supply the organization with the wherewithal to produce can also have power in so far that they can control the volume and nature of supply, yet a number of suppliers exist, all eager to do business. At other times the power base may shift and a supplier may only want to enter business agreements if certain preconditions regarding volume or costs relative to total purchases are met.

## 4. Bargaining power of buyers

The buyer usually has a great deal of power. Apart from the ability simply to walk away from the deal, the buyers can judge their ability to influence the vendor by analysing the volume of the vendor's goods that they purchase. If the volume is large, then by going elsewhere they can have a major impact. But in addition to this obvious power, the buyer's power will also be based upon how well informed or how profitable the buying organization is itself, or upon its ability to use substitute products and so on.

## 5. Threat of substitute products or services

The threat of substitute products or services displacing your own can affect both individual organizations and whole industries. What determines the threat can be the relative availability of substitutes or a major change in their price (this is often the result of changes in technology), a switch in the cost structure within a market and then, of course, the degree to which buyers feel inclined to substitute different products. Some of these threats can be very difficult to avoid and are outside your control. However, if relationships between seller and buyer are good, if the service always remains excellent, if efforts are made to maintain the most effective methods of communication, then perhaps the threats can be minimized. So, an overall philosophy when establishing a strategy must be to strive always for excellence and to over-communicate rather than under-communicate.

There are, of course, other components within each of the five forces but the above is hopefully enough to give an overall idea of the depth of discipline and analysis required. Powerful though it is, it is unlikely that any one person can do justice to this approach and this is both a strength and a weakness within it. It is an externally focused instrument and therefore contrasts with the final tool of analysis – the balanced scorecard approach.

## The balanced scorecard

This concept is largely a measure of performance but as such is a useful catalyst for action. It arose out of a growing sense of dissatisfaction with the idea that the only way to analyse the health of an organization was through financial measures such as return on investment. It became generally accepted that, in order to achieve lasting success, organizations should adopt a more balanced approach to measuring performance by considering a wide range of performance measures. The concept of the balanced scorecard, devised by Kaplan and Norton (1992), is probably the best method of integrating the various criteria that combine to make for success.

The balanced scorecard came about as a result of a research project conducted with 12 companies who were considered to be leaders in 'performance measurement', and from the study Kaplan and Norton devised a set of measures to give top managers 'a fast but comprehensive view of the business'. They expanded their definition, stating that their scorecard allowed managers to look at the business from four different perspectives and that it set out to provide the answer to four different questions which were allied to them:

1.  How do customers see us?              Customer perspective
2.  What must we excel at?                Internal perspective
3.  Can we continue to improve and        Innovation and learning perspective
    create value?
4.  How do we look to shareholders?       Financial perspective

A strength of this approach is that while it gives managers information from four different perspectives, it limits overload (with its consequent reduction in focus) by limiting the number of measures used. From the initial analysis, a number of goals and measures can be derived against each of the perspectives and so both vision (right brain) and control (left brain) are built into the approach. As such the balanced scorecard approach is much more than a measurement system; it is also a management system and, more than that, it is the basis for both strategic direction and action.

Kaplan and Norton acknowledged that their scorecard had to be tailored to each different company that adopted the principle, otherwise managers would spend their whole time striving to resolve conflict between objectives that did not complement or balance one another. They stated that, 'The balanced scorecard is not a template that can be applied to businesses in general or even industry-wide. Different market situations, product strategies and competitive environments require different scorecards.' In saying this, Kaplan and Norton are being extremely modest, perhaps unrealistic, as to the usefulness of their approach as a strategic tool. Many organizations have adopted the scorecard as a useful means of analysing their overall health and as a starting point for strategy-making. So, to say that the scorecard needs to take existing strategies into place demeans it as a tool of strategic analysis. Indeed, it has become the basis for a number of initiatives based around the concepts of strategy and operational excellence, one of the most notable being the British Quality Foundation (see Figure 3.3) which has developed the business excellence model and allocated percentage points to various attributes indicating the extent to which they contribute to the overall concept of organizational excellence as measured by the Foundation.

The model tells us that customer satisfaction, employee satisfaction and favourable impact on society are achieved through leadership that drives policy and strategy, people management, management of resources and processes; all of which combined lead to excellent business results. It is a splendid template from which large-scale strategies can be formed. In Figure 3.3, the enablers are concerned with how results are achieved while the results are concerned with what the organization has achieved or is achieving.

There are many other tools for assessing the strategic health of your organization and from this analysis developing a competitive strategy. Several of them make you look at your markets and your products with a view to the future exploitation of

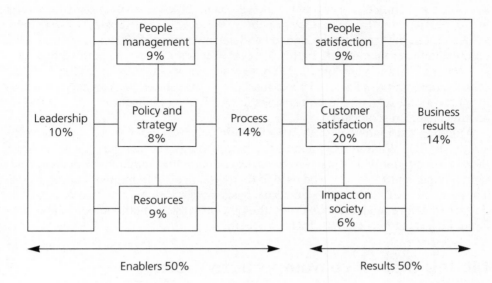

*Customer satisfaction, People* (employees) *satisfaction* and *Impact on society* are achieved through *Leadership* driving *Policy and strategy, People management, Management of resources* and *Processes*, leading ultimately to excellence in *Business results*. Reproduced with permission of the British Quality Foundation

**Figure 3.3**    **The business excellence model (*Source:* Reproduced by permission of the British Quality Foundation)**

both. For example, there is Ansoff's matrix, the Boston Consulting Group's growth–share matrix which forces you to look at your relative market share and then there is the multifactor portfolio matrix which requires you to analyse your business strength against various factors that might make an industry attractive to be in and from there force you into decisions about your position in the market, ranging from invest through harvest to divest (get out of). Some of these tools are described in Chapter 5. As a mature strategist, as with so many other areas of knowledge, your skill should be to know where to look for a tool rather than knowing them all off by heart.

So, which of these tools of organizational health analysis should you use, and when? They all ask a fundamental question: 'What is my firm's relative competitive position within the industry, what are its key strengths to exploit its position and how can I use them to improve that position?' The core test of any tool is whether it fits our definition of strategy, namely:

> The process of adopting a new mindset, of surveying the overall situation, of focusing on a goal and making the hard choices necessary to achieve it.

Clearly all methods described above help you to look at the situation facing you.

The five forces model, for example, allows you to look at the situation from a very broad perspective. Some models, such as the core competencies model, help achieve focus but from a more defined and narrow perspective, while some can be completed faster than others. In the end, it is necessary to use the method that best suits your situation, your knowledge base and your own talents. In so far as many models, ranging from Porter to benchmarking, were conceived as an aid to marketing, I favour those that take a more holistic look at the organization such as SWOT and the balanced scorecard.

Although the models described so far help you to achieve focus, they are less strong on the 'What comes next?', the hard choices and actions that flow from them. Consequently, the final two tools described below, although basically problem-solving instruments, can be used to focus you in on action rather than analysis. They can be used either on a standalone basis or as a follow-on to one of the tools described above and are powerful, thought-provoking methodologies that can either be used alone or debated within a team.

## Models that move from focus to choice

Two of the most effective models for moving you from analysis to implementation are those of demands, constraints and choices and then force field analysis.

### *Demands, constraints, choices*

This method was derived by Rosemary Stewart (1982) and explained in her book *Choices for the Manager*. She was concerned that managers were too driven by the here and now; all they saw were demands upon their time, and a host of problems that made it difficult for them to address these demands. Consequently, they worked flat out, seldom seeing the wood for the trees and seldom acting as real managers in so far that they often did not stop to think about the choices of action that were open to them. In short, they were at best tactical, seldom acted as planners in anything other than the shortest term and were never strategic. To help managers overcome this conundrum, she harnessed the various forces affecting managers in such a way as to turn them into benefits rather than problems. The model works like this:

#### Demands

Think of all the demands facing you. A demand can be summarized as a 'must' – something you must do, otherwise you will be sacked or your business will run into major, perhaps terminal, problems. This is because an accurate list of demands should define the future strategic direction of the organization. A list of demands might therefore look something like this:

- Ensure profits are made
- Make an impact in the industry
- Delight customers and satisfy stakeholders
- Improve the structure of the business
- Ensure quality of the product or service
- Initiate new sales drive
- Update and innovate
- Ensure staff morale remains high

... and so on.

## Constraints

These can be summarized as anything that acts to prevent us achieving the demands; not surprisingly they are often felt more keenly than the demands themselves. A list of constraints would probably include many of the following:

- The culture of the organization
- Motivation level of staff and fear of change
- Actions of competitors
- Inappropriate technology
- Wrong budget levels set
- Lack of our products' differentiation from those of competitors
- Lack of awareness of our brand in the market
- Level of buyers' bargaining power
- Legacy of past mistakes in price setting

... and so on.

Of course, the challenge does not lie in analysis but in *what to do with the analysis*. And it is here that we can move into the more creative area of choices.

## Choices

These are exactly what they seem. They are the ways by which you can elect to 'bust' the constraints in order to meet the demands. As such, these actions in themselves move us towards achieving the strategic goals. At one level a choice may be simple. You may elect to do some things differently, to ignore some constraints, to select between alternatives, or at times quite simply just to say 'no' to some demands that may not be reasonable. At another level the choices are more complex; they could involve:

- Selecting between buyers
- Choosing to discontinue a (currently) worthwhile product
- Deciding to compete in one segment of a market rather than another
- Investing in new technology even though cash is short

- Changing the image or brand
- Agreeing to develop a new competency
- Taking steps to retrain staff to meet new demands
- Changing the structure of the organization.

In this model, it is the choices that are the most important. They can dictate strategy and they can dictate tactics. Above all else, the model lends itself well to team meetings, to brainstorming and to debate. We choose to act and it is the actions arising out of the making of choices that both set and implement the strategy.

## Force field analysis

This is a methodology rather than a model and is usually used to look at and solve a problematical situation. As a methodology, it incorporates a number of steps and, for it to work properly, these steps must be followed in the right order. The steps are reproduced below but before going through them we need to look at why the whole process is called force field analysis.

In any situation involving change or movement (and strategies are all about change), a number of forces will exist. There will be forces for change, called driving forces, and forces that mitigate against change and in favour of retaining the *status quo*, called restraining forces. Force field analysis is all about identifying these forces and harnessing the energy for change inherent in the situation in such a way that it overcomes the inbuilt inertia or force of resistance to improvement. As such, this methodology incorporates the philosophy of some of the more sophisticated martial arts. The essential steps of force field analysis are as follows:

### Define the problem

1. Describe your present state, the problem as it appears to you, and try to describe your feelings about the situation.
2. Describe the desired state. To do this describe the situation as you would ideally like it to be. Try to use more than one statement to describe what you really want.

### Analyse the problem

3. List the restraining forces that are acting to maintain the *status quo* or actually making things worse.
4. List all the driving forces that can be brought into play to help you to move from the actual to the desired state.
5. List both the driving and restraining forces in order of importance.

## Develop solutions

6. Brainstorm and list the possible action steps to help get rid of or reduce the importance of the main restraining forces.
7. Do the same for those action steps likely to improve the positive effect of, or help make happen, each driving force.
8. Select the most promising action steps. It may well be difficult to do everything so select the most promising actions generated in steps 6 and 7 and start to think what to do about them.

## Develop a plan

9. List the action steps and for each step list the resources, people or budget required to carry out that action.
10. Draft the overall action plan. To do this look at all the actions noted or already implied. This should include making timetables, schedules and allocating responsibilities to those who will carry out the actions.
11. Review the plan. Try it out on a colleague. Find out what the obstacles or objections to it might be and discuss where it could go wrong. Having done this...
12. Write up the plan and make a start.

Like demands, constraints and choices, force field analysis lends itself to teamwork and brainstorms. It can be used together with the discipline of demands, constraints and choices in so far that you could identify certain constraints, look at the choices open to busting them, move on to the difficulties inherent in trying to bust them and then apply force field analysis to analyse and overcome them. This does, however, lead us on to the question of what tool or technique to use and when.

# The right tool for the right occasion

Henry Mintzberg, in studying a wide range of managers, found that their days could be characterized by three words – brevity, variety, discontinuity. By this he meant that most of their time was spent doing short jobs and that those short jobs did not bear much relationship to each other in terms of content and the demands they made upon the individual. Finally, he felt that the way these short varied tasks hit the poor managers meant that there was a great deal of discontinuity in their days, one thing did not flow smoothly on from another and therefore both concentration and effective time management were difficult.

So, to coin a phrase, 'You pays your money and you takes your choice!' Time will be short but it must be found! Some tools will be faster and easier to use. SWOT analysis, for example, can be done relatively quickly and simply, as can the task of working through demands, constraints and choices. Others will require more time and preparation; force field analysis, for example, usually takes a lot longer than anticipated and benefits from a team approach. Then there are those that not only require a team approach but also necessitate considerable prior research by those taking part – identifying core competencies, choosing benchmark organizations, defining the criteria to build your own balanced scorecard, are all cases in point.

A further element in helping you to decide what tool or technique is most applicable is that of identifying where you are at in the five-stage strategy process model. As a guide and summary, this is reproduced here (see Figure 3.4), giving the stage, the strategic questions to be asked at this stage and the tools most applicable for taking you successfully through that stage.

| Action | Topics | Question |
|---|---|---|
| Analysis | SWOT, marketing mix, benchmarking, balanced scorecard, critical success factors, people and team health | Where are we now? Where have we come from? |
| Formulation | Creativity, brainstorming, developing intuition, 2005 scenario planning | Why do we want to do it? Where do we want to get to? |
| Evaluation | Criticality, force field, demands, constraints and choices, lessons of previous acquisitions, etc. | How are we going to get there? |
| Implementation | Staff empathy, emotional cycle of change, positive and negative aspects of change, overcoming resistance, leadership, stopping slippage | How do we do it? Whom do we do it with? |
| Control | Action plans to be recorded, behaviour change contracting, accounting systems to be evaluated | How do we know that we are getting there? |

**Figure 3.4    A strategic route map – the full picture**

# Moving the plan forward – control

Of course, once the models have been worked, the key element of being strategic is that of action, of implementation, of getting things done!

This is where down to earth planning takes its place, assessing who will do what, identifying how to tell that it *is* being done. Identification of key elements of the plan is vital and control is of the essence. Each and every plan must be different and tailored to address the demands of the situation in question. For example, force field analysis is an excellent tool for planning but does not guide you through the minutiae of the planning process. To help with this, I have set out a number of typical features of an implementation plan below. In illustrating the following sample process one factor, however, will always remain true – it is necessary to plan the plan!

## The plan: typical elements

1.  Develop possible alternative sequences of action
2.  Decide on the most promising sequence
3.  Develop priorities of sequence and major steps
4.  Identify the jobs and tasks that make up these steps
5.  Look to see what resources, people and monies will be needed to implement them
6.  Anticipate what could go wrong and build in contingency actions
7.  Determine how progress will be measured

Once again, you should be able to see how the stages of the plan resemble the overall strategy model, which in turn resembles the process used in creating your own creativity, explained in Chapter 2. It is merely a matter of degree and angle of focus – fractiles are at work again!

And how do we really know that we are getting there? In Figure 3.5 I have illustrated the closed loop of feedback and control. Here the feedback given to you, as supplied by accountants as a means of achieving hard objective measurement, is vital and the information, in order to be truly useful, should be specific and tailored to meet your needs. If this is not the case, then as with so much that is supplied by accountants it will be voluminous, accurate, but unread and of little use. When I was a line manager with Plessey Electronic Systems Limited I was continually confused and frustrated by the volume of financial data served up to me for supposed reading and analysis on a monthly basis. I was being swamped with facts, which although relevant to the business did not affect my department. Eventually I made a deal with the finance director; he would edit the information to the effect that I would only be given facts concerning my department's budget or facts that might impact upon industrial relations within the business. I for my part would stop complaining and agree to read what was given me!

# Conclusion

Finally, how do you pull the whole thing together? How do you set out to conceive the strategy, plan the plan and establish the controls? Few business strategies are born in isolation; if they are they will either be flawed or the leader will have a harder job to convince others. Strategies should be the product of teamwork, of debate, sometimes of conflict, but always of pooled energy. Consequently, at this stage, I have added a model of a short strategy formation workshop. Starting by sharing participants' Herrmann brain dominance profiles, it allows those present to understand how each may be able to contribute to the strategy and to shine at a particular stage of the process. However, it is not intended to be an exercise in navel gazing as it swiftly moves on to action and implementation. I should also add that the following outline programme is intended to give an idea as to what can be done but does not go into sufficient detail to enable anybody other than a skilled facilitator to run it.

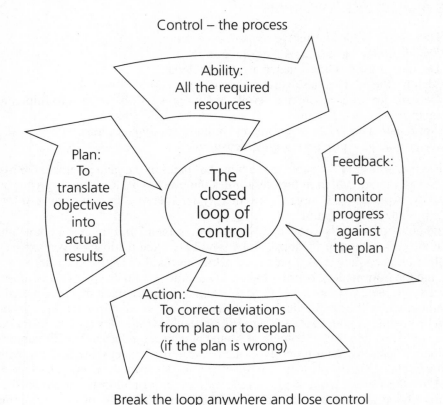

Control – the process

The closed loop of control

Ability:
All the required resources

Plan:
To translate objectives into actual results

Feedback:
To monitor progress against the plan

Action:
To correct deviations from plan or to replan (if the plan is wrong)

Break the loop anywhere and lose control

**Figure 3.5    The closed loop of feedback and control**

## Strategy formation workshop

*Objective*

To build a strategy by using the talents of the executive team and put plans in place for the implementation of that strategy.

1.  *Analysis*   As an executive team, what are our respective strengths? Use of the HBDI to examine both the individual and overall orientation of the team. Does it have the complementary strengths for strategy formulation and decision-making?

2.  *Formulation of strategy 1*   What are the issues we face? How does the environment we work in affect us? An examination of the demands, constraints and choices encountered by members both individually and collectively – where do they place us?

3. *Formulation of strategy 2*   Where do we want to get to? What is our vision for the future?

4. *Evaluation*   Does the vision with its implied goals make sense? How can it be refined? What are the implications for us all in terms of our accountabilities and future actions?

5. *Implementation*   What will our first steps be? What leadership style will be most appropriate?

6. *Control*   Getting there? How will we know that we are getting there and what could go wrong? In attempting to implement this vision, what could stop us? Selection of one or more problems and use of force field analysis to find solutions.

7. *Further plans*   Participants work on and share their own plans for making the strategy happen and discuss their responsibilities as a team.

The length of this workshop has been left open; some of the questions could provoke lengthy discussion and if a target duration has been agreed then a facilitator may be necessary to ensure that the team sticks to timetable. In producing a generic example of a team-based strategy workshop it does presuppose that the team will work well together. This may well not prove to be so, in which case it is doubtful whether much of any lasting value will be achieved. One criterion that will help to ensure a successful and productive event will be if the team is able to buy into a common vision of the future – without it most strategies will appear meaningless and most leadership directionless. Consequently, having now defined what being strategic means, we will actually go back a step to look at the fundamental prerequisites of vision, mission and values.

## Action points for consideration

- Adopt a model of strategic health analysis and try it out on your own organization. What does it tell you?

- Identify an organization against which to benchmark your own. What does it have that your organization does not have? What can be learnt from this? What can be done?

- Consider the various sources of power within the market in which your business operates. How is it placed?

- Identify the demands, constraints and choices which face your business and also you as an individual. Making choices may well imply risk, but can you afford not to make them?

- Consider the extent to which you have built in a range of checks and controls that will enable you to plan your plans and control them once action starts.

- If you are a member of a board, or run a team, think about setting up a workshop in order to facilitate a better understanding of your situation as well as formulate a direction towards identified goals.

# Chapter 4

# From vision to strategy

Many years before people started to talk of business strategies or of strategic visions, Jonathan Swift put the whole subject into perspective. Vision, he stated, 'is the art of seeing things invisible'.

Much has been spoken and written about the importance of vision; it has become a trendy concept. This is unfortunate as being trendy implies transience and the concept of the vision transcends time and puts the façade of fashion into the shade. If people had not had visions in the past, to put it bluntly, the human race would not be where it is today. In fact, it could be argued legitimately that it would not have progressed far beyond the Stone Age. Fire might exist as a fortunate but accidental discovery and mankind might have learnt how to wear the skins of the beasts they ate in order to provide warmth, but there would be little else to show that we were the prime intelligence on the planet. And so mankind's ability to display vision, along with the restlessness, the impatience and ambition that accompanies it, has been a crucial factor in achieving the gigantic leaps of progress from the Stone Age, through the Machine Age, to the Information Age to . . . ?

If man can be characterized as a machine-using animal, then man can equally well be described as a 'vision-needing' persona. But how do we describe this strange characteristic? Here is a short case study to help answer this question.

In 1997 Great Britain went through a number of major changes. In a remarkably short period of time a new government was elected, referenda were set up to establish new parliaments for both Scotland and Wales – and then the country had to contend with the death of a princess. Indeed, so cataclysmic was the culmination of these events that *Time* magazine set out to analyse the situation, contending that the Prime Minister and the Prince of Wales now had to chart a new course for both Britain and its monarchy. It quoted Susie Orbach, who had been Princess Diana's therapist, and who commented on the fervent emotions expressed before and during the funeral: 'What has happened didn't just start last week. There's something of the mood of May's election in it: something about the nation wanting to articulate anew what it stands for.' The article concluded that 'when Diana died, the people spoke but what they said is complicated: as the majesty of her funeral proved, Britons still want the orchestra to play *Pomp and Circumstance*. They just want to toss a little Elton John into the mix'. A telling picture of a nation realizing that it is on the threshold of major change but not fully knowing what the change should be or where it should lead them. A nation in need of a guiding vision to show the way forward and be the mother of strategies for progress.

So whatever the situation, be it the case of a country in transition or an organization facing up to the demands of a changing business environment, a vision is essential. Also essential is the need to define it accurately and analyse more closely the role it plays in making strategies happen.

## Visions that have changed our lives

Where we all are now, the way we act, the way we think, the way we organize our beliefs and ethics, the way we apply them in our personal and working lives (including how we actually get to and from work), are all the product of someone's vision and the subsequent strategies that made them reality. Visions can be dangerous as well as the most marvellous phenomena known to mankind, just as a lack of vision can be the greatest threat to business, civilization and even the planet. An overview of just a few of these visions should be more than adequate to demonstrate this point.

There is an old saying that in 'polite society' at any dinner party with people whom you do not know well, three subjects are taboo: sex, politics and religion. So, let's add the topic of business to these three taboos and look at where powerful visions have transformed our lives in these respects. In fact, there are so many examples in each of these fields that it is only possible to look at a token sample – a sample, however, that will hopefully prove the point.

### Sex

If you look at how people behave or talk and especially at what they believe, compared with how they thought and acted, not just in Victorian times (which have become a byword for both primness as well as hypocrisy) but also in comparison with how they were just a few short decades ago, the changes are immense. I am not talking so much about the areas of personal morality as that of the role of women.

Although there is still much talk of the glass ceiling and although there is still some way to go before women can truly claim equality across the board, the changes in Western societies since the 1960s have been immense. Women now are approaching parity of numbers with men in most of the major professions as well as in the field of business management and, if we look at the statistics coming from Western educational systems where they are consistently outperforming their male counterparts, will shortly be overtaking them.

The reason? This phenomenon is not so much a product of the educational system as of the vision of a few influential women who initially set out to make other women re-evaluate themselves as sexual beings, but ended up making them rethink their entire role in society. While in the 1950s the Kinsey report undertook a detailed survey of sexual mores as they existed at that time, Germaine Greer in *The Female Eunuch* challenged women with a vision of what they could be to fulfil themselves in terms of their whole being as women, mothers, workers and professionals. The vision implied in the metaphorical challenge of 'burning your bra' turned out to be far more significant than was originally implied by this trivial act!

## Politics

The field of politics and history abounds with visions and their products. The following examples are but a few fairly recent ones from the twentieth century. Hitler developed a perverted vision for Germany based upon the emergence of a Third Reich that reflected a Wagnerian view of society coupled with a desire for territorial expansion encapsulated in the phrase *Lebensraum* – room to live, room in which to be true Aryans! Facing him across the English Channel, Churchill countered with rhetoric that painted a stark picture of a grim struggle that would nevertheless end with a glorious victory, 'There will be blood, sweat, toil and tears; but we shall never surrender . . . And if the British Empire should last for a thousand years they shall say – this was their finest hour!' In the US, Martin Luther King led the civil rights movement with the clarion call of 'I have a dream', and more recently Tony Blair set out to develop a vision for the UK Labour party under the flag of New Labour. On the other side of the world, in Malaysia, Prime Minister Dr Mahathir developed and published a very specific vision for his country with the intention of turning it into a fully industrialized power by the year 2020 – not surprisingly, he called it Vision 2020.

## Religion

This is an area where visions abound and have done so since time immemorial. Both the Christian and Muslim religions are based on the visions or revelations of their founders and both founders used graphic symbolism portraying wonderful future states as eventual outcomes of keeping the faith. Much of the visionary symbolism often used in both business and politics has been inherited from the Christian faith. Since then, the founders of sects and of bogus religions have often used the tactic of articulating visions to draw in followers, sometimes with tragic consequences.

Better this, however, than the ridiculous assertion of a Scandinavian business guru that visionary terminology should be confined to the realms of religion and the arts. In fact, visionary language is not only appropriate but necessary in the fields of business, commerce and strategy generation, a phenomenon that I will examine for the remainder of this chapter.

## *Business*

Once again, the pool of examples is huge and business leaders have been using visionary language long before the term became popular. In pre-industrial Britain, James Watt experimented with the power of steam and then harnessed his dream of a new source of power into creating the steam engine – the age of mass transport had dawned. Much later, Walt Disney was to say, 'What I see in the distance is still nebulous but it is big and glittering', a half-baked vision that was later to be consolidated into the might of Disney films and Disneyland; before this his vision was 'To create a place where we can all be kids'. Other organizations in other industries have boasted different visions. British Airways set out to be 'The world's favourite airline', the Schindler Elevator Company set out to move from being a leader in manufacturing to a 'Leader in a service industry', Sony articulated a future state in which Japanese manufacturing would lead the world in terms of innovation and excellence with Sony at the vanguard of the movement. And so on … The business world is full of visions and vision statements, perhaps even more than the worlds of politics and religion – perhaps because it is in even greater need of them. In my study of middle-ranking business leaders (van Maurik, 1997) all the leaders I interviewed had clear visions of what they wanted to achieve for their organizations – among a diverse, international collection of people it was one of the common themes!

So, without doubt, the initial vision sets the long-term goal and thereby points the direction to be followed – a direction that the strategy will unfold in such a way as to make it happen. If the vision (which in itself is part of the strategy formulation) points to the *where* we must get to, the strategy uncovers the essential *how*. If there is no vision how can you generate the motivation that will help complete the strategy? First of all you engage the heart, then the minds and feet will follow.

But this whole area of strategy formulation is fraught with misunderstandings and with confusing definitions. Companies use words like vision, mission, values and purpose in such a way as to confuse most people and thereby defuse their strength. The one word mission has been used to define the end goal, describe the strategy process and also to define the essential *raison d'être* of the organization itself. At the same time value statements and vision statements have often become interchangeable. General Electric USA stated 'When teams succeed, individuals get rewarded.' Is this a business goal or just a desirable state to be in? Unless the meaning of key definitions is sorted out, they will only breed confusion.

## Clarifying definitions

Perhaps the clearest redefinition of the elements of vision that make up the components of strategy was made by J. C. Collins and J. I. Porras in the *Harvard Business Review* (1996) and I have taken some of their excellent terminology and blended it with some ideas of my own to stress how a clear separation and distinction of key components is essential to business success.

Collins and Porras state that an organization must have a *core ideology* – this is something that defines the enduring character of the organization. It is an identity that transcends short-term product or market cycles and is in effect the glue that holds the organization together. However, as this is a somewhat nebulous concept, it can be broken down into *core values* and *core purpose*.

## Core values

These are the essential truths in which the organization believes. They are sometimes not clearly articulated but are nevertheless strongly felt. Indeed so powerful are they that individuals who do not ascribe to them seldom last long. For example, the core values of a religion would be the key beliefs of that religion. If you decided to believe in something else it would not stop you being religious but you would probably have to formally switch religions, or at least switch churches. So, a value is 'Something to rate high, to esteem, to set store by'; values are resistant to change and they guide our actions. Different organizations, of course, have different values; Boeing has a core value of 'Making aircraft we would be proud to put our families on', Sony has a value of 'Do not imitate', while the Disney Corporation has a value of 'Imagination and wholesomeness' – whoever saw a sex scene in a Disney film – go to a different company if you want to make the sequel to *Basic Instinct*!

So core values are connected to fundamental truths. In his poem *Truth*, John Masefield saw the part truth plays in forming our collective consciousness and in initiating action:

> Man with his burning soul
> Has but an hour of breath
> To build his ship of truth
> To sail on the seas of death
> For death takes toll
> Of beauty, courage, youth
> Of all but truth

(Reproduced with the permission of The Society of Authors as the Literary Representative of the Estate of John Masefield.)

## Core purpose

This is the organization's reason for existing; it is what it is there to do, it is also what it stands for. Sometimes the core purpose is called the mission but this term can be confusing. The core purpose reflects the essential reasons for doing the company's work. For example, the core purpose of my organization, PA Sundridge Park, is 'To help client organizations through management development and training'. The core purpose of our parent, the PA Consulting Group, is that of 'Creating Business Advantage' for its clients. As Collins and Porras (1996) say, an effective core purpose is like a guiding star, for ever there, for ever pursued, but never reached. You can act in accordance with a purpose, you can comply with it, but it is too big and enduring to be accomplished. A good test of your core purpose is to ask, 'What would be lost to the world if our company ceased to exist and why is it important that it continues to exist?'

And then there is the vision itself.

## The vision – stretching goals for the future

Without the vision, there is nothing! It is the leaven that makes the bread rise, the catalyst that starts the chemical reaction, the starter motor that kicks the high-performance engine to life. It is the key to action, implementation and results – the paintbrush that gives the subsequent strategy shape, form and purpose.

But what exactly is it?

The vision is quite simply the desired future state for your business, your department or division within it – or perhaps even your life! It can be expressed in words and it can be expressed in pictures. Whichever way it is expressed, it must, however, be put over in a way that excites and motivates other people because the vision will be describing a future state that has not yet been achieved. Getting to it may be difficult, may be stretching but getting there is vital. Consequently, the way the vision is expressed must convey both the challenge that the future state implies as well as the excitement of getting there. Collins and Porras (1996) call their definition of the vision 'big hairy audacious goals' (BHAGs) and this conveys something of the stretch and excitement implied in a true vision in that it must genuinely convey a picture of a desirable future state.

Examples of strategic visions abound and several have been described earlier in this chapter. They are often described in pictorial form and one high-level team build that a colleague and I ran for an IT department serving a major company formulated a vision for their future in which they saw themselves as pilots guiding other functions within the organization (these other functions were represented by ships in a stormy sea) towards a safe harbour (see Figure 4.1). The stormy seas represented the effects of non-integration of IT policies, while the safe harbour illustrated the benefits of all functions operating in the same way and relying on that IT function for ongoing advice and support. This not only clarified their role but enabled them to quite literally paint a picture that described accurately what they should aim to become in the future.

In the field of politics (and after all what arena is more suitable for both visions and grand strategies?), Tony Blair set out to communicate a stretching vision, a BHAG if ever there was one, to the first Labour Party Conference following the party's election victory in 1997. In the past Blair had been accused of sloganism because of his sound bites containing business language about 'a stakeholder society'. Now he stated that he wanted his administration to be 'One of the great radical reforming governments of British history'. He went on to say that to achieve this would mean hard choices as it would need to be a compassionate government with a hard edge – 'a government of high ideals and hard choices'.

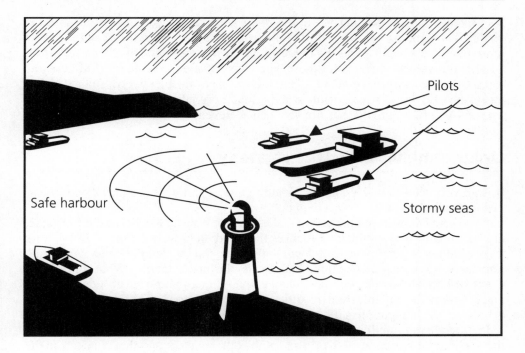

**Figure 4.1** **A strategic vision in pictorial form**

Having set the scene, Blair set out his real vision for the country. Britain, he stressed, could be 'The model nation for the twenty-first century; a beacon to the world'. With passion in his voice he reiterated the vivid picture that was driving him, 'We can never again be the mightiest, but we can be the best!' Somewhere, amid the evocative tones of Elgar's *Pomp and Circumstance*, could be heard the pulse of a new beat; was it the rhythm of Elton John or something yet more demanding? Blair went on to underpin his vision with a strong value statement. Family values would be at the core of everything his government would do and he concluded with an appeal to the nation to join him in the march towards the vision, 'Give your all! Make this the giving age.' Perhaps it was not the voice of Elton John that could be heard in the fire and passion of the vision, but an echo of William Blake's glorious hymn, *Jerusalem*:

> Bring me my bow of burning gold:
> Bring me my arrows of desire:
> Bring me my spear: O clouds, unfold!
> Bring me my chariot of fire
> I will not cease from mental fight,
> Nor shall my sword sleep in my hand
> Till we have built Jerusalem
> In England's green and pleasant land

It is interesting to note that while the press and public acclaimed Blair and his vision, its reception by rank and file Labour Party members in the conference was reported as 'lukewarm'. Was the message too strong, too much of a departure from Old Labour values? A shock for those who were satisfied to settle for mediocrity as a price for achieving socialism? Certainly, looked at objectively, Blair's vision meets the acid test of a real vision in so far that it is challenging and that it portrays a desirable future state that has not yet been achieved.

## Linking the vision to the strategy

It is all very well to understand one's core purpose, know the values, have a clear vision. But how do you make it happen?

If the act of conceiving the vision makes you look ahead to a desired future state, the subsequent strategy-making focuses the mind on how to get there. But getting there requires organization right down to the most minute detail. Grand visions and impressive strategies are one thing but 'the devil is in the detail!'. What is needed is a way of logically connecting the vision to everything that must subsequently take place within the organization in order to make it happen. The best method of achieving this integration is through what I call 'the visionary eye' (see Figure 4.2).

Pictured here is an illustration of the cross-section of a human eye. At one end is the part that looks out on the world and at the other end the part that connects to the optic nerve and sends the messages to the brain that cause us to respond to what the eye has seen.

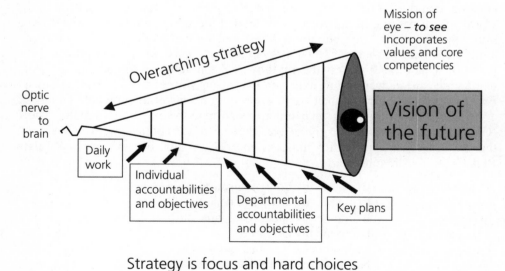

**Figure 4.2**      **'The strategic eye'**

The core purpose or mission of the eye is to see. That is its reason for being and without it we would not be able to get from A to B without great difficulty. The fact that the eye can see in the first place enables us to move forward. However, the eye looks ahead and sees a desirable place to reach – the vision. It is now necessary for us to work out how to get to that place. At this stage the physiological connection becomes strictly metaphorical, but if you imagine that the lens of the eye focuses back down towards the optic nerve, then that focus becomes the overarching strategy. The strategy then causes a number of major plans to be made; these plans may cut across divisions or may integrate with them, it does not really matter at the moment – what does matter is that these major plans (which when integrated become the stuff that the strategy is made of) will influence the accountabilities and objectives of departments and functions within the organization.

At this stage it is necessary to digress and talk about accountabilities and objectives. An accountability is something for which you have a long-term responsibility or something you will have to answer for one day. For example, if you are a sales manager, you will always be responsible for sales; you will also probably be responsible for the morale of the salesforce and for keeping clear channels of communication open with the production and product design functions. As long as you are in that job and as long as the job specification is not drastically altered, these will be your long-term accountabilities.

On a shorter-term basis, you will also have objectives. These are places to get to by a specific time. They will be detailed and quantifiable. For example, as a sales manager you may be given objectives such as increasing sales by 20 per cent by the end of the financial year, undertaking a review of morale among sales people, recommending various training programmes for them in order to address any issues, and setting up regular monthly meetings with production and product design in order to ensure that your salesforce do not make promises to customers that the company cannot meet. As the old saying goes, objectives should be SMART – specific, measurable, agreed, realistic and time-related.

So functions and departments should be given accountabilities and objectives that line up with the strategy; they should be geared, or altered if necessary, towards supporting its implementation. At the same time, individuals within functions and departments will be given personal accountabilities and objectives that not only line up with those of their departments but, by the same token, will support the overall strategy itself.

Consequently, the daily work of individuals at any level within the organization should therefore support the implementation of the overarching strategy. This is because the daily work end of Figure 4.2 is the place where the hypothetical optic nerve connects to the brain – the place where the strategy is driven forwards! Sometimes the nature of the work, or its very existence, may be called into question in lining it up with the strategy, but that will be just one of the hard choices that may need to be made. If everything is properly integrated, the strategy will be implemented in a timely and effective manner. It should, therefore, be possible to look at the daily work of anybody within the organization and to pose the acid test, 'Is this work contributing towards the fulfilment of our strategy?' If it is not, change it!

To describe this in theory is one thing, to actually make it happen is something else and that will call upon your skills both as a leader and manager; attributes that we will examine in Chapter 7. However, before that, we need to look at the actual process of both creating and testing out your vision.

## Creating your vision

Few of us are blessed with the equivalent of a 'road to Damascus' experience. A moment when the future is mapped out clearly for us in a sudden blinding moment of truth. For the majority, any inspiration with which we are blessed is most likely to be made up of 95 per cent perspiration! Yet our visions for the future can be created and the process of doing so can be an all-embracing and stimulating experience. What follows is not a blueprint, as both visions and the process of creating them can be very personal as well as specific to different situations; rather it is a series of hints and broad guidelines.

The first step is to be relaxed and to clear the mind. Creating your own vision is in itself a creative process and you should bear in mind the hints about paradigm busting, personal space for creativity and jamming described in Chapter 2. Having cleared a space – both mental and physical – start the process. All visions start with desire so ask yourself this fundamental question. What do I really want for the organization/function/department? From this should stem the following questions:

- What do I want it to look like in the future?
- What will it feel like to work for it?
- What will it be like to do business with it?
- How do those who may consider themselves to be stakeholders in the business regard it and what might they want for it?

Let yourself freewheel as you consider the options and in doing so you will probably come up with some essential desires that can be expressed in terms of size, shape, method of operation, markets to be in, projected future turnover and so on. For some people this process is best started by doodling, actually drawing what you want the vision to look like. If the vision is being created by a team (and this is more likely to produce a balanced and democratic picture in itself), a useful process is for the team to go through a pile of glossy magazines and to produce a collage of vivid images representing the desired future state from the pictures they find in them. The picture that may emerge could be that of a more efficient organization, with a highly focused product range, operating in a fully international arena with branch offices in Europe, the Americas and South-east Asia. If this picture seems realistic, it can then be put into words.

The vision statement should describe where you want to get to, what it will be like when you have got there and also indicate the time-frame or target date for doing so. A typical vision statement might well read something like this:

Our aim, by the end of the decade, is to become the world's most sought-after training consultancy, delivering exceptional results to our clients and operating on a truly global scale.

After that, you can start to sort out the details. To do this, it will be necessary to take each major component of the vision statement and to test it with the following simple but demanding questions. If we apply the discipline of these questions that follow it should then be easy to break down the example vision statement into its component parts and to subject each to challenge and scrutiny.

- *'The world's most sought-after'*   What does this mean? Can this be measured by the amount of business we are doing or by the number of enquiries we receive? Does it mean that we will be able to pick and choose who we do business with? Can the statement be reflected in the variety of organizations for whom we work? Does it imply a future campaign of publicity and networking?

- *'Training consultancy'*   Once again, what do we mean by that? Are we fully in that line of business or are there new skills and competencies that we should adopt to more accurately reflect that description? If so, what actions are implied?

- *'Delivering exceptional results'*   Can they be quantified as well as qualified? How will we know if what we deliver is regarded as exceptional? How will we approach our clients to find out? What internal standards will we apply? Does it mean we will need to go for ISO certification?

- *'On a truly global scale'*   Is this a different statement from 'The world's most sought-after' or have we fallen into the trap of rhetoric? Does it mean that we will be actively engaged in taking our business across the world to our customers rather than them coming to us, and if it does mean that, what are the implications for our organization's human resource function?

In going through this simple yet demanding process you will have started to sort out for yourself exactly what your vision for the future will be, as well as how it can be expressed in terms of numbers, future goals and future states. Some actions may already be implied, but resist going into detailed planning at this stage – the *how* forms the strategy and it is too early to focus in yet! When playtime, in other words the fun side of vision creation, is over, it will be time to get down to specifics.

At some stage, you will probably have had to abandon the pictorial vision and concentrate on the written statement; now the question of how lengthy to make that statement will arise. Some vision statements are so short or unspecific as to be virtually useless. British Airways' old vision of 'To fly to serve' may have helped its staff focus on the idea that it should become the world's favourite airline but it was pretty useless at helping people to concentrate on targets or on debating what differentiating qualities the company would aim to adopt. Other vision statements are far too long. For example, in 1991 Dr Mahathir, Prime Minister of Malaysia, published his Vision 2020 – a vision of his country as a fully developed technological nation by the end of the first quarter of the twenty-first century. The document is over 6000 words long – a worthy and challenging concept but so lengthy that most

Malaysians can only give you the broadest outline of what it says and certainly cannot give specific examples of the targets within it.

So the exercise of creating your vision for the future of your business, function or department will have been a vigorous one. In the end, there is only one acid test for both the vision as well as the process of creating it. Does it excite you? To be more specific: can the goals be described as big, hairy or audacious? Was the process invigorating? If the answer to either question is 'no', then try again. For anything to be motivational it must engage the head, the heart and the feet. The vision statement must engage the head, must stand up to intellectual scrutiny; but if it does not engage the heart then the feet will never be put into action – nothing will ever get done and no strategy will be put into place. Tom Peters tells the story of how he challenged one organization to have a compelling vision of how it could regroup in order to deliver compelling customer service levels. 'Why should we have one of these vision things?' complained the CEO, 'We're no worse than anybody else.' 'Go shout it from the roof tops then,' challenged Peters, 'We're no worse than anybody else – that's our strap line'! There was no reply!

## Examples of driving visions

You certainly do not have to be at the head of a large corporation in order to create and act on strategic visions. The following examples are of people who started in a small way but whose visions have, in their own particular ways, made a difference.

### Colonel Mark Cook

A new charity is on the scene and it is changing the lives of hundreds of children throughout the world. The source and inspiration for this charity comes not from a large organization with an army of aid workers but from a single individual with a burning vision for the future.

Mark Cook was a professional soldier with a broad-based experience in many theatres of soldiering who suddenly found himself chained to a desk, doing an office job that did not appeal, and at the same time finding that he did not share the vision of his bosses. Consequently, when the Army offered him the post of commander of the British contingent to the United Nations forces in the Balkan War, he jumped at the chance of doing some real soldiering again. It was during his time in the former Yugoslavia, as commander of a peace-keeping force that had its hands tied in so many ways, that Mark Cook came across a very real tragedy and from it found himself challenged in a way that forced him to develop a new vision for both his life and his future employment.

The challenge sprang from the thousands of children whose lives had been wrecked by the conflict; children who had been orphaned, whose homes had been destroyed and who now lived in cellars to escape the bombardment or who were quite literally locked up in squalid orphanages. The plight of these children appalled the tough soldier and the indifference of those in authority to their sufferings disgusted him. Cook vowed to do something about them and took action as soon as he could, persuading his soldiers to give up their free time (with large bribes of beer, he adds) in order to rebuild a house for some of the worst affected children to live in. After the success of this venture, the germ of something bigger, better and more challenging began to grow in his mind. Would it be possible to start a venture that set out to give homes to children whose lives had been blighted by war and then to make this happen anywhere in the world? From this challenging question, Mark Cook developed the concept of a charity that would do just that – where there was suffering and despair it would seek not just to build homes, but to give hope. From this vision was born the charity 'Hope and Homes for Children' – a vision of an organization that would build where war had destroyed and of an organization that would always go one step further than appeared to be necessary.

What followed is now comparatively well known. This is not the place to go into the complex strategy involving publicity, fund-raising and the mind-boggling logistics of establishing building projects in war-torn areas. What does need to be stressed is that it was the power of the tangible vision of a viable and effective charity that made all the other activities possible, giving them purpose and drive. Hope and Homes for Children is now a well-established and growing charity that is rapidly becoming well known and meeting its growth targets. However, as long as wars create hardship and homelessness, the vision will always be pertinent.

## Guy Black – Aero Vintage Ltd

If you were to visit Guy Black's home in the south of England, the first thing you would notice would be a large Russian tank parked in the front drive. Black would explain, rather apologetically, that it came as part of a deal when he bought an extremely rare Second World War German tank in a museum of tanks and military vehicles; he desperately needed that tank to fill an important gap in a national collection. In fact, he had to buy the whole museum and had tanks of all nationalities littered all over the place in both Kent and Sussex, with most finding new homes in other collections throughout the world. A few favourites remain in his own collection!

So what is this all about and how did it start? As a child, Guy Black developed a keen interest in finding out 'how things work'; he was the kind of boy who would take things apart and put them back together again for the sheer fun of it. At the same time his father, who was a major influence on his life and who had been a pilot in the RAF during the war, fostered in him a keen interest in racing cars and old aircraft, especially those of the Second World War and earlier. Black grew up in a childhood era of popular wartime heroic stories, further romanticized by an early memory of his father, while on a camping holiday, showing him a flight of RAF Spitfires overhead. 'This is the last time you will ever see these historic aircraft flying together in the skies,' his father prophesied. Guy Black determined that this would not be the case; a lifelong passion had begun at the tender age of eight.

As an adult, Black became an engineer and found himself too much of a rebel to sit comfortably within most large engineering firms. He was too proud of the engineering and technical excellence that had been the hallmark of earlier generations, and was therefore critical of what he saw to be the de-skilling of engineering workforces, and he worried that there would come a time when people would lack the manual skills to create excellence with their own hands. Having started a company restoring historic racing cars, which grew so large as to be almost out of control, he sold it and turned his attention to old aeroplanes, determined this time to keep the operation at a manageable size. He was able to combine his wish to preserve the history of aviation as a living, flying entity with his desire to see the continuation of old but still relevant skills. His desire developed into a vision of an organization which would seek out old, derelict and crashed historic aircraft, restore them to flight capability and then sell them on to the museums of private collectors. It would employ and maintain the highest engineering skills and his people would learn those skills, keeping them alive for future generations while at the same time making an ongoing contribution to aviation history.

Since then, his organization has flourished. Although deliberately never allowed to grow large enough to dilute its founder's vision, it has contributed significantly to the stock of historic aircraft and tanks (another passion) around the world, setting the highest standards of authenticity, engineering and conservation. Guy Black has sourced, from all four of the most obscure corners of the world, aircraft and military vehicles of the rarest kind – often unique survivors – ranging from a rare Bristol Fighter from the First World War to a group of unique 1930s Hawker biplanes, a German Fiesler Storch (of the type used by the Germans to rescue Mussolini from the invading allies at a resort high in the Abruzzi mountains of central Italy), a unique surviving Russian YAK-1 from a Siberian freshwater lake, another German tank from a Russian swamp and, of course – and not least – his childhood obsession, a Spitfire.

Every year, Guy Black puts on a private air display and gathering of vintage aircraft at his own airfield, Old Hay in Kent, for his staff, their families and, of course, his own friends, as an assembly of the best in flying history and technical excellence; it is an occasion not to be missed! So, once again a vision has led to a strategy that has created an organization, which in turn has created employment and added value. Without the vision and the desire to accomplish what must have at one time seemed like unattainable goals, Guy Black, like Mark Cook, would probably never have succeeded. And without their differing contributions, the world would probably be less compassionate, less fun, less colourful.

## Checking that the vision is valid

So how do you know that your vision is relevant, that its lofty aims can be commuted into a viable strategy? And once you have started to implement the strategy, how do you know that it is working?

These, of course, are the 'crunch' questions. There is an old saying: 'An action without thought is not very much; a thought without action is nothing at all'. Consequently, it is vital to know whether the vision is:

a) transferable into targets and actions; and
b) whether progress towards them can be monitored.

Whereas vision creation is a right brain activity, the checks and measures to ascertain whether it actually is happening are strictly left brain. It is all too easy to conceive of something so fine, so audacious that practicality goes out of the window – and then, of course, the critics have a field day.

For example, the ambitious Vision 2020 for Malaysia has already been cited as a powerful and ambitious goal for this fast-developing nation. Part of the job of making the vision happen involved the establishment of a high-tech super corridor outside Kuala Lumpur, a $40 billion plan to build something to rival California's Silicon Valley which therefore would catapult Malaysia to the forefront of both trade and technology. The huge corridor was planned to be 50km in length with the world's tallest building at one end and a massive new airport at the other end. Alas, a number of unanticipated factors acted to threaten this strategy in the latter half of 1997.To realize this dream not only would the government have to complete one of the most formidable construction projects in history but also change the country's attitude to everything from the use of foreign workers to the prickly problem of censorship – cyberspace after all can bypass local morality with a single click on a mouse. The high-tech corridor has therefore been seen as a threat to traditional values by the increasingly influential and conservative Muslim hierarchy. In addition, currency speculation on the Ringit exposed weaknesses in the Malaysian economic system and helped reveal what *Business Week* (1997a) described as 'politically connected crony capitalism' which it claimed involved insider deal-making by a political elite where 'friends' were rewarded with public works projects and overseas contracts. Dr Mahathir's angry reaction to the financial speculators was then seen as threatening to foreign investors which in turn exacerbated the crisis and generated the comment that 'Malaysia's entire economic strategy must now be re-thought'. *Business Week* asked the crunch question: 'Is Malaysia just high-tech dreaming?' The truth is that to turn dreams into reality means that all the internal and external influences on that dream must be taken into account when formulating the strategy.

If governments can lose their way, it is even easier for businesses to do so and businesses seldom have the benefit of being deluged by public comment and advice. Here are a number of vision check questions to help you ensure that the essence of the vision stays alive, vibrant and relevant as the strategy unfolds:

1. Does the vision really illustrate what I want to achieve?
2. Is it relevant to this type of business?
3. Is the vision clear? Can it be communicated in a way that will convince and excite other people?
4. How will the vision mobilize others? Are there any clues?
5. How will the vision be translated into a series of objectives that other people will want to adopt as their own?

6.   Can the vision statement along with the essential values it conveys be reflected in everything we do and be a yardstick as well as a guide?

In order to prevent a vision from becoming 'pie in the sky' it should be tested against questions such as this – the more vigorous the testing, the more robust the vision!

# Conclusion – communicating the vision

For the vision to mobilize strategic thinking, for it to energize others, it must be communicated. Herein lies the key to both success and failure. It is likely that those at or near the top of an organization will have better access to information than those lower down and should therefore find it easier to define the vision. However, total reliance on one's self as the boss to generate the vision can probably be the biggest mistake you can make. If you approach your staff as one coming down from the mountain with the vision carved immutably on tablets of stone, a likely reaction may be short-term excitement followed by subsequent disillusionment or rejection. The reason? Those who are to be involved in making it happen have not been involved in forming it. In order to cause something to be done enthusiastically and willingly it is necessary to touch both the head and the heart; after that the feet will follow. The heart will only be evoked if people feel that their views, hopes, fears and aspirations have been accounted for in constructing the vision of and pathway towards the stretching future state.

If we take an organization to be similar to a mountain with different people standing at different levels on that mountain, certain analogies can be made. At the top of the mountain stand senior managers (the strategists), halfway up the mountain stand middle managers and specialists, while at the base stand more junior people. Halfway up the mountain there is a cloud and this cloud cuts off the senior managers from the middle rankers and the middle rankers from the most junior. Furthermore the cloud means that those at the top can see into the far distance, but not down the mountain, while those at the bottom can see all the rocky places at the base of the mountain, but not the summit. Those in the middle, as is so often the case, feel that they are perpetually in the fog while at the same time having demands made on them from above and below – the challenge is to somehow disperse the fog so that all can share the vision, see the possibilities and enjoy the challenge of new opportunities. Sensitive consultation combined with insightful communication is the key.

So, when allowing yourself to dream listen to your heart, use your intuition and also relish the insight that facts and knowledge can give you. An anonymous sage once wrote 'Knowledge is the organ of sight, not the eyes!' So gather knowledge, allow it to liberate your inner eye to give it powerful long-range vision as well as the ability to communicate it. The vision that has emerged and been accepted may generate powerful changes, may instigate progress and, certainly as part of progress, should pave the way for innovation.

# Action points for consideration

- Develop the art of 'seeing things invisible' – take the time to conceive a vision.

- Allow those working with you to develop the vision with you – subject it to the power of teamwork.

- Consider your organization's (or indeed your own) core ideology. To what extent does it govern decision-making?

- Check, if you have a common vision, whether it is mirrored in everything that is done in the organization. Use the vision check questions to do this as well as to check the validity of the vision itself.

# Chapter 5

# Innovation and marketing

'The only source of competitive advantage is continuous strategic innovation.' Thus said Costas Markides, and since he said those words the pace and level of innovation in the world of business has continued to increase at an ever-quickening pace.

Indeed, it could be argued that while some businesses are started to provide established and well-known goods or services to markets that already know what they want, it is those other businesses that are started to provide something new, something that the world does not know that it wants, that have the greatest chance of breaking records of growth – or of disappearing for ever without having made any impact at all. By the same token, those businesses that are able to examine critically the way that they produce, to press continually for new products or methods of production or delivery, are those most likely to grow and prosper. It may be possible to survive for a while as a high street florist, or as a jobbing plumber – in both cases providing the tried and tested for those for whom short-term gratification is of prime importance – but even in those cases will that prove to be enough? Whether we are gadget-infatuated teenagers or even staid octogenarians, there is something in the human spirit that enjoys new things, is intrigued by novel ways of doing the old and which holds a sneaking admiration for those ingenious people who are able to apply their intellects to improving what is already in existence. Sometimes these people are mocked – the cliché of the 'nutty professor' is a common one – but do we not often mock that which we do not fully understand, that which we might secretly fear? In a special report on transformations within Silicon Valley, *Business Week* was quick to acknowledge that it had also transformed the world around it, both technologically and culturally. And of the Valley's leaders? With some irony, it stated, 'In high school we called them nerds. Now we call them millionaires.'

So the pickings are potentially enormous – in the same way that the pitfalls for not adopting an innovative mindset are horrendous and gape ominously in the path of us all – plumbers and florists included! Lampikoski and Emden (1996) in *Igniting Information* stated that economists had concluded that 'innovation and increased information account for 60 per cent of the competitive improvement in the economy of any country, while only 40 per cent derives from direct investments (in new production facilities or sources of raw material)'.

But what exactly is innovation? How do we recognize it or define it?

## Innovation – our inescapable legacy and duty

The results of innovation are all around us and while it is impossible to separate the concept of innovation from that of change, they are in fact separate entities. The one will lead to the other, while at the same time change is likely to take place independently of any innovative developments that may be taking place. For example, the cost of computing power is known to drop approximately 30 per cent every year while at the same time microchips are doubling in power every 18 months. We all know that your computer is obsolete by the time you buy it and that computer companies are terrified of renting them to you as you would continually be hounding them for replacements and updates. Paradoxically, computer power is now 8000 times less expensive than it was 30 years ago and more available to an even greater extent. As John Naisbitt (1994) commented in *Global Paradox*, 'If we had similar progress in automotive technology, today you could buy a Lexus for about $2. It would travel at the speed of sound, and go about 600 miles on a thimbleful of gas.'

While not many of us would want the mythical Lexus car with all its capacities, it most certainly would have a number of advantages – environmental for a start! However, instead of the mighty Lexus, we see the effect of the staggering rate of innovation within the computer industry all around us in the massive changes it has caused in both our work and domestic lives. Even in the 1970s about half of all workers in the industrialized world were involved in manufacturing of some sort or other. Pundits predict, however, that by early in the new millennium, no developed nation will employ more than 15 per cent of its workers in traditional forms of manufacture. The growth of the service sector has been fast and this growth has impacted not only on organizations such as banks, accountancy firms and the like, but also on types of organizations that traditionally saw manufacturing as their strength. A main feature of this landslide from manufacture to service has been the fact that *knowledge* is becoming one of the most important competencies of an organization; perhaps even a product in its own right.

But what good is knowledge as such? There is no point (apart perhaps from the mental satisfaction) of having great knowledge of the physiological working of the brain if you do not apply it. It is when the knowledge is put to good use, when it is made to solve problems, to grow new areas of knowledge or to create novel products, services or approaches, that it really comes alive. It is then that we can truly start to talk about innovation.

So what then is innovation? Innovation is not knowledge, it is not even creativity. It is, however, the product of both. Moreover, innovation is in no way knowledge added to creativity; at the very least the defining sign for this equation must be a multiplication sign! Innovations may come about as a result of a road to Damascus blinding flash of the obvious. However, they are far more likely to be bred from the hard work of creative people using their knowledge in ways that cause the multiplication sign to work and who then concentrate on applications and methods of implementation. The concept of innovation is in many ways a paradox – it is a method, a result, but chiefly a necessity! Furthermore, an innovation does not have to be an entirely new product or service; it can arguably be the adaptation of something already in existence to add value – that in itself can be extremely creative and many mind-boggling innovations result from the creative adaptation of an existing concept or idea.

Being innovative is not an option. If in the past it was the weak who went to the wall, now it will be the uninnovative, or perhaps being uninnovative will be the new definition of weak. In 1997, Bill Gates of Microsoft set out to convince US cable companies to let him design a new set of set-top boxes for digital TV. His design included a high-speed cable modem that would enable users to 'cruise the world'. The box would combine the functions of a cable modem and a digital set-top box in one device, it would use Microsoft software and be far cheaper than current cable modems. The industry was intrigued; adoption, moreover, would give Gates control over the TV set in much the same way that he has control over today's PCs. So, innovation is about power, control and success. But how do you make it happen? How do you make it both an integral part and product of your organization's strategy?

## Sources of innovation

To use a procreative analogy: a creative approach is the parent, knowledge is the seed and innovation is the child. However, before conception is achieved, an elaborate courtship must take place; both the atmosphere and the attitudes of all concerned must be right. In short, you cannot simply say to people 'Be innovative – get on with it!' That would be akin to rape. No, the process of stimulating innovation must be a thoughtful and sensitive one. If you wish to compare it to seduction, then the most successful seductions are based on careful planning, creation of mood and a careful analysis of what will turn the other person on. But before any of the above can take place, the opportunity must be spotted and must not be wasted.

### *Opportunities to innovate*

Innovate or die. Extreme situations such as war or national crisis have created an environment where innovation has leapt ahead at a staggering rate of knots. Sometimes the innovation has come about as the result of hard, concentrated graft, as was the case with the amazing technological advances in radar, sonar and ship design that enabled the Allies in the Second World War to overcome the menace of U-boat wolf packs and win the Battle of the Atlantic. In other cases the great leap forward has come about as a result of the ingenious adaptation of something already in existence. To stay with the Second World War for a final example: the US Air Force was suffering heavy losses over Germany due to the fact that no fighter had the range to escort B52s to their targets and back. US Mustang fighters potentially had the range but not the power to fight successfully, British Spitfires had the power but would never have the range. Result – stalemate. This impasse was eventually broken when one engineer had a blinding flash of the obvious – put Spitfire Merlin engines into Mustangs thereby making them overpowered and capable not only of outfighting German Messerschmitts but also of carrying the extra fuel tanks to make the long journeys that the 'raids' entailed. In both cases there was an urgent need and in both cases those involved were opportunistic. So what are the key opportunities to innovate?

The most obvious conclusion is that those who wait for the pressure of necessity are likely to be the last in the pack. Peter Drucker (1994) in *Innovation and Entrepreneurship* has made one of the most thorough analyses of the opportunities or sources of innovation. Some of the most pertinent which can be most easily linked to a broad-based strategic question are outlined below.

### Unexpected success

When something goes right when it was not expected to do so, very often nobody stops to analyse the real reasons. There may be short-term euphoria and congratulations but nobody stops to ask why or to assess what can now be done to capitalize on the situation; perhaps no mechanisms were in place to deal with the success? The key strategic questions here must be:

- Why did we succeed?
- What can we learn from this success?
- What gems can we capture before they fade?

### Unexpected failure

Failures are much more likely to be noticed and questions to be asked (unless there is a 'strategic cover up'). It is when no real error can be found that questions most need to be asked, as previously unnoticed changes may be occurring in the market or operating environment. These changes could represent a threat – or preferably an opportunity. Strategic questions here are:

- What can we learn from this?
- What may be changing out there?
- What does it mean to us in terms of research, knowledge or learning?

### The unexpected outside event

Developments such as a changing pattern of demand outside your immediate business area may present opportunities. There may be some way in which your organization's existing competencies may be directed at this new opportunity without fundamentally changing the type or nature of your business. In short, is there something out there that is temporarily 'up for grabs' – is there a window of opportunity? Strategic questions here are:

● What is going on out there, what has changed?
● How could it be relevant?
● What could we do?
● How long have we got?

### Incorrect assumptions about reality

Drucker (1994) says that many opportunities to innovate arise from incongruities. For example, when managers make incorrect assumptions about reality, they are likely to direct all their efforts in the wrong area. This may make things worse, not better, and it is easy to lose contact between cause and effect. To overcome this threat, it is necessary to look at how systems are operating in the market and where the opportunities really lie. A key threat often exists in producers and suppliers misconceiving what it is that the customer actually buys. For example, as they believe deeply in their products, it may involve a considerable paradigm shift to recognize that the customer actually values and is buying something else. The mindset may be 'We produce the highest-quality product, we are valued for this'. In fact, the customer may in reality be buying service and may shift allegiance if the supplier is perceived as arrogant. Strategic questions here are:

● What assumptions have we made?
● What do people really want from us?
● What implications exist for us in terms of design or approach?

### Processing the need

There are many needs which are widely recognized but for which no solution is currently available. For example, the first person to find a surefire antidote to AIDS will unleash a hurricane of demand. This is an extreme example, but there may be other needs that are not so obvious and, in the absence of a solution, everybody carries on. However, the opportunity for innovation occurs when the solution arrives or grows closer and someone remembers the need – or finds a way of moving a partial solution towards that need, conceivably to find and exploit the missing link. Strategic questions here are:

● What is relevant? What does the world need?
● What has changed recently in terms of our product or services?
● When did we last really look at potential linkages?

### Indicators of impending change

Changes may occur rapidly in markets, industries or economies and to take full advantage there are four indicators of impending change. (1) Rapid growth: this will have an effect on the structure of an industry as well as the methods and processes within it. (2) Doubled volume: this will inevitably have an effect on the way that industry leaders segment the market. Finally, (3) converging technologies and (4) changes in the way of doing business will also provide fertile opportunities. Strategic questions here are:

- What signs of change are observable?
- What signs of new knowledge are there?
- How can we move to exploit them?
- Where are new technologies most evident?

Drucker (1994) also points to changes in the mood and perception of overall reality of the general population as providing big opportunities and, as this is a harder area to quantify as logic plays a far lesser role here, the risks are greater. For example, the population's overall health is far better than it was a few short decades ago yet people worry more about their health. This may be illogical but there are tremendous opportunities for innovation here.

On the other hand the major question is, 'To what extent is this a long-term trend or a mere fad?' The dilemma here is that if you wait too long to quantify your perception, you may well find that you have missed the bus; on the other hand you may have tried to add value to something that was short-lived. Either way, you can strike it big or have invested time, energy and money unwisely. There is no easy answer, as the man from Decca Records who rejected the Beatles with the throw-away comment that 'The days of guitar-based groups are over' soon found out. If ever there was a case for combining the strength of focused A- and D-brain thinking, this was it and the necessity of doing so clearly remains for us all.

So in our metaphorical seduction, once the opportunity has been identified, it is then necessary to create the right atmosphere.

## Creating the atmosphere; generating the mood

As in all situations of this sort success depends on getting a number of different components into place. One component on its own is less likely to work than when it is taken alongside other components which can then be very powerful. To conclude the analogy: soft music alone is unlikely to guarantee success, but when taken in conjunction with the right lighting, good wine and privacy – who knows what might happen . . .

### Make time

It was George Bernard Shaw who quipped in a letter to a friend, 'I am sorry that I have written you such a long letter. I did not have time to write you a short one'. Many a true word is spoken in jest! It is one of the great truths that while a minute proportion of the population are capable of genius under any circumstances (I imagine that Shakespeare could probably have written *Hamlet* while travelling to work on the Underground if circumstances had demanded it), for the rest of us creativity, inspiration and that added inspiration of what to do with the initial inspiration require time and space. People who are continually pressured to achieve deadlines, sales or utilization targets – or whatever other indices of productivity that sterile bureaucracy forces on them – are unlikely to find either the time or motivation to be innovative unless it is in ways of trying to beat the system.

If the main thrust of the organization's work lies in piecework then it makes sense for people to work flat out. But this is decreasingly the case these days; people work with information, interpret knowledge and sell concepts. For them to be good at this, to come up with new ideas or improvements, they need time to think, to debate and to create. They need time to network, to argue and to reinvent. In short, they need time to play! When I worked at Plessey Radar, which at that time was at the forefront of systems technology for radar systems, my boss (who was one of the old school) was constantly irritated on walking through the engineering design offices to find people sitting back and staring at the ceiling. 'And they tell me they are working!', he would snarl. That is in fact just what they were doing! Fortunately, my boss had the insight to realize this although it still went against the grain for him not to see people poring over their drawing boards.

## Create skunk works

This expression refers to a place, often a designated room or office in an organization, where people can gather to think up new ideas.

Frequently there is something rebellious and underground about innovative people, it is part of their love of challenging the obvious. The trick is not to crush this rebellion but somehow to institutionalize it but not, by so doing, defuse it. The answer lies in creating somewhere, an office, a 'common room', where people can get together to share knowledge or opinions in an informal and unforced way. This common room may be untidy and unoffice-like (hence skunk works), that does not matter. What does matter are the outputs emanating from it.

Sometimes the skunk works become embedded in a group of people who usually share the same office or area. There should be no rules and no externally imposed productivity targets. The only external input should be that any ideas arising will be noted, listened to and, wherever possible, given a fair trial. In his song *Love minus zero. No limit*, Bob Dylan wrote and sang about the energy generated in informal encounters where people read, debate and sometimes even draw their conclusions on the walls. It is often the conclusions that are drawn on walls, scribbled on the back of envelopes or on the proverbial 'fag packet' that are the most important, the most original – the most innovative.

## Grow knowledge

A lot has been published about the learning organization and it is certainly not the intention here to reiterate the arguments for promoting the wish to learn among everybody in the organization, and the subsequent desire to convert that learning into first-rate products and services. But, to put it very pragmatically, where do you start?

The first step must be one of analysis. What skills, knowledge and talents do your staff have? During my years in the world of work, from getting to know people in organizations as diverse as carpet yarn spinning mills to firms of chartered accountants, I have been constantly amazed at the range of skills and interests that people have exhibited; sometimes these skills have been closely linked to their core areas of work but often they have been entirely different. I have known a partner in a major firm of accountants who built his own house, an engineer who was a renowned astrologer and an export clerk who was a world expert in ferns, with several species named after him. The essential fact is that all the skills, knowledge, attitudes and opinions of an organization's people are relevant – the people are the organization's greatest asset so that what constitutes them is vitally important. The tragedy is that most firms do not know what their people are good at apart from the narrow range of activities that they are employed to perform. The first step must therefore be to ask them, to make lists of the talents and then to see how they can best be deployed.

After logging the skills and knowledge, the next step must be to grow them. Apart from skills-based or management training, there are many ways in which it is possible to widen the field of vision of those working in the organization. Visits to other organizations operating in the same markets, fact-finding missions to suppliers and customers are all important as are organized visits to trade shows and ensuring that staff continue their professional development through involvement in their professional institutes. The range of activities by which people can grow their levels of knowledge is enormous; the key strategic skill is then to analyse how best that range of skill and knowledge can be deployed to increase the organization's innovative agility.

## Emphasize the OK behaviours

All too often the most challenging or innovative people in an organization are regarded as eccentric – clever but non-promotable! Consequently, many essentially innovative people decide that it is more profitable to toe the party line, or to seek managerial paths to the top rather than to emphasize their innovative (and sometimes unconventional) talents and opinions.

A particularly potent example of this was illustrated some years ago when I worked for Plessey Electronic Systems. Our division had a large engineering function of over 300 people and the organization structure had several management grades; there were, however, only three major jobs in the function with the result that many well-qualified and talented engineers felt that they had nowhere to go in career terms. In order to put this situation right, we set up two alternative grading schemes to the managerial stream that was already in place. It was now possible to work one's way up through a technical grading scheme or a commercial scheme. In all schemes, managerial, technical and commercial, the grades were the same but it was now possible for individuals to work their way up through their engineering or commercial knowledge rather than through having to hold managerial responsibilities. This opened up new routes to high pay and benefits and was designed to relieve career frustrations. To our surprise, many of those assigned to the technical or commercial streams initially complained as the mindset that stated that the only way up was through being a 'conventional manager' was deeply ingrained. It took many meetings and nearly two years before the scheme became truly accepted and began to produce the win–win situations it had been set up to achieve.

Another way to encourage innovation is to make it not just acceptable but desirable to encourage conventional wisdom within the organization. Too many people have original thoughts but are afraid to voice them. With this sort of atmosphere prevalent it is most unlikely that an organization will achieve any breakthrough innovations. It may well be able to achieve incremental improvements in product or processes – but will these be enough? No, to achieve radical breakthroughs three factors must be allowed:

1.  The organization must make a public statement that it values diversity of opinion and approach and must subsequently back this statement up through its actions. Creativity is often encouraged by the initially abrasive nature of diversity. Somehow sparks are made to fly and when the abrasion moves towards consensus, the spark is still there but has somehow become focused into a steady, illuminating flame.

2.  It must be seen to be OK to fail. One successful organization asks all its staff at appraisal time to identify one failure on their behalf. It is only when they cannot identify a failure that they are criticized as this means that they have avoided risks, have not tried to be innovative!

3.  Ideas must be given a hearing, someone must listen to them. Suggestion schemes may abound but if ideas disappear into a black hole then the scheme has been worse than useless. Indeed, if it became the case that everyone who submitted ideas would have the opportunity of discussing it with a senior executive – and of being listened to! – then perhaps more would come from schemes such as this. All too often organizations hire in consultants to tell them what their own people could have told them. Perhaps it is something about 'A prophet not being without honour except in his own land'. Nevertheless, organizations should take better advantage of their own internal prophets/consultants – of their own people's voices crying in the wilderness!

But now we are really starting to talk about the organization's culture.

## Create the right culture

In the end, culture is all about how the people in the organization feel about it, the extent to which they are able to balance the need for self-expression with the ability to contribute to excellence and innovation through the membership of teams. A survey conducted in 1997 of what employees expected from their employers indicated in ranked order of importance:

- Interesting, challenging work
- Open, two-way communication
- Tools/opportunities for growth and development
- Realistic performance management
- Secure employment
- Work versus 'other life' balance
- Involvement in decision-making
- Performance-based pay
- Equitable benefits
- Non-monetary rewards.

A closer look at these factors makes a clear link between people's basic needs and the desire to be innovative. We could look at it in terms of Maslow's hierarchy of needs: the basic needs for survival, food, shelter and acceptance have been satisfied in many employees – especially those who are by implication more talented or creative – consequently their key needs are now at the top of the hierarchy of needs; we can see a strong need to create, to grow and to have one's contribution noticed and appreciated. Some of the smarter organizations have noticed, noted and acted upon these needs before they were made explicit via surveys and reports and these are some of the organizations currently regarded as trailblazers. There is, for example, an uncanny similarity between the top ten factors and the six key criteria that Dr William Coyne (1996), Senior Vice-President of research and development at 3M (an organization widely heralded as being one of the most constantly and tenaciously innovative in the world), has stated as being necessary to sustain continuous innovation. The six major requirements are:

1.  Have a vision for the future and make it widely known and explicit.

2.  Have foresight based upon an understanding and anticipation of customers' needs – both the needs they are aware of and also those they are not yet aware of.

3.  Set stretching goals. As innovation is 'time sensitive', whether it is based on customers' current or emergent needs, it is always necessary to act quickly. Innovations and products must be introduced that 'redefine what is expected by the customer and that leapfrog the competition' (Coyne, 1996).

4.  Hire good people and then trust them. This could be regarded as just another 'motherhood and apple pie' statement were it not for the fact that technical

employees at 3M are allowed to spend up to 15 per cent of their time on projects of their own choosing. The organization is happy to institutionalize a bit of healthy rebellion in their labs on the basis that this has in the past led to some dynamic innovations, including the now legendary Post-it notes. This does not mean to say that 3M encourages total anarchy; pressure to 'think customer' still remains. Out of the 60 000 products developed by the organization, all (including 450 derivations of the original Post-it note) were developed as a response to an individual need from a customer.

5.  Encourage open and extensive communication. The organization recognizes that ideas and discoveries will spark off more ideas and discoveries. In order to add impetus to this tendency, 3M holds technology fairs, organized and managed by the technology people themselves to promote networking and the cross-fertilization of ideas.

6.  Recognize and reward innovation. This does not come in the form of huge bonuses for work done, as people are in fact doing what they were employed to do. However, there are a variety of institutionalized non-monetary awards which include the possibility of election to an elite group of top 3M researchers and also the ability to choose between opting for promotion into either management or more advanced technical positions, both of which offer the same benefits in terms of salary and other benefits. The scheme that took some time to get going within Plessey Radar is obviously alive and healthy within 3M.

3M, despite its fame and reputation, does not have the monopoly on either innovation or on the ability to create a culture that will support it. At Oticon in Denmark, an organization that makes hearing aids, Lars Kolind (Labarre, 1997) has helped to build up a business model and organizational culture of considerable daring – and success!

Kolind is adamant that hearing aids are not what the company is really about. He states that it is really about the way that people perceive work – it is about giving people the freedom to do what they want. And this freedom has generated astounding success as, in a world market for hearing aids that has been flat for some time, Oticon has more than doubled in size and operating profits are almost 10 times their 1990 level. A further yardstick of the company's success, or perhaps the main reason for it, is that the company has introduced 10 major product innovations, including the world's first digital hearing aid. But how did this all happen? What liberated the organization?

The answer lies in chaos. It was Tom Peters (1987) who first identified the concept of thriving on chaos and this is one organization that genuinely appears to do so. Kolind set up an organization with the minimum of organization but one where the main driver was the project – he wanted each project to feel like a company in its own right and for staff to 'feel liberated to grow personally and professionally, and to become more creative, action-oriented, and efficient' (Labarre, 1997). Within the chaos of disorganization, projects were set up as the key element of work and any good idea that was able to attract people to it became a project.

In order to maximize the creative churn, Oticon has dispensed with formal offices, desks and paperwork; people have to move around because owned work space does not exist and this means that people do not think in terms of formal departments and they also network much more effectively. Out of the chaos, the abrasion of teams forming and re-forming, has come the most effective interchange and use of knowledge together with high levels of creativity. This, in turn, has led to a huge impetus for innovation. It is organization, structure, hierarchy and bureaucracy that are regarded as the enemy and one of the key functions of top management is to keep the company disorganized. Indeed, Kolind has stated that he is so convinced that this is the case that he has been known to institute large-scale reorganizations when he sees project teams in danger of becoming formal departments.

# A model of culture and empowerment

So, how can the lessons from organizations as different as 3M and Oticon be distilled into something that can be used to help other organizations formulate strategies of communication, culture and organization that will enable them to have the flexibility, the knowledge and, above all else, the will to be innovative? In so far as the disorganization within Oticon was part of a long-term strategy, and the marathon creativity within 3M is part of such a long-term strategy that it has become imbedded within the organization's value system, so all organizations should examine their prevailing cultures to ensure that they meet the demands of the business environment that they face. It is here that a more formal definition of both 'empowerment' and 'organizational culture', both as terms and as tools for enabling innovation to take place, may be useful.

## *Empowerment*

Like many management expressions, the word empowerment has become overused, misused and, in fact, a devalued currency. It is widely regarded as a 'good thing' in much the same way as, in the broader theatre of life, physical exercise and the consideration of others are regarded as good things. But what do we mean by that? Does exercise mean undertaking the rigours of a weekly marathon and does consideration mean giving half your worldly wealth to the poor? Or do they mean something less demanding, both physically and spiritually?

So many different definitions of empowerment exist that it would take far more than the scope of this chapter to even scratch the surface. Instead, I will give a short pragmatic definition of my own. Empowerment is what the leader or organization does to enable people to work as happily, independently, creatively and above all effectively as possible. To achieve this three elements must be in play:

**Challenge – Support – Autonomy**

Challenge is necessary. It provides the stretch that adds the sense of excitement to get people going. Sometimes it makes people work to prove something to those challenging them and that is no bad thing in itself!

Support is vital as people will rise to the challenge far better if they know that there are ways of obtaining help and advice, if they know that in the end there is someone there to listen to them. If you feel abandoned, the temptation to give up or to blame the system for your impending failure is very seductive.

Autonomy is another crucial ingredient and one that in no way contradicts the others. People do like to do things their way; in their personal lives they are often used to making significant decisions about finances, relationships and purchases, but when they get to work often they find this freedom is severely curtailed. As the Chinese philosopher Lao Tse declared, 'When the good leader's work is done, his people will say – we did this ourselves!'

So what does the good leader then do? The job is simple. Have your antennae constantly at full extent and be ready to adjust the level of each major element at any time. But there is more to it than that. The good leader should craft the culture of the organization to maximize the benefit of each factor and in doing so should be aware that there is a process to be gone through and a definite, desirable goal – the growth and improvement of the business.

## Three levels of organizational culture

Some of the most valuable work in the field of organizational culture has been produced by a consultant, Roger Harrison, who has identified three forms of culture, transactional, self-expression and mutuality, and he asserts that they exist as a hierarchy through which most organizations will evolve. The problem is that it is all too easy for an organization to slip back to its previous state, usually as a result of unenlightened leadership.

### Transactional cultures

The first stage of evolution, transactional cultures are usually very hierarchical and are characterized by high degrees of command and control. Motivation is achieved by stick and carrot, reward and punishment while individual behaviour is controlled by multiple rules and regulations. Consequently, people compete with each other for power and status. There is an immediate impact on the strategies of such organizations; they tend to be oriented towards quick gain and profit and may well react to events rather than anticipate them with new initiatives. Arguably, this has been the prevailing culture for the majority of organizations over the centuries but it can also be argued that if an organization is to succeed in the new millennium, it must grow out of this mode.

## Self-expression cultures

These are much more autonomous and egalitarian in approach and encourage the individual to help them achieve a share of, or make an impact in, the marketplace. Consequently, individuals in cultures such as this will be rewarded for their individual, sometimes individualistic, contributions to success or product development. There is usually a high level of internal competition in these organizations, usually centred around such observable entities as the achievement of sales targets or personal initiatives centred around product development.

This approach will fit with any firm's strategies in the marketplace that are experimental and high risk. Rewards will be high for the successful, especially where a direct link can be drawn between their efforts and an observable achievement by the organization. The atmosphere, however, is very often that of sink or swim, dog eat dog, although many people who work within self-expression cultures are happy to do so because it fits with their own ambitions.

## Mutuality cultures

Harrison describes this as the most mature form of culture – the final stage of evolution. It is best characterized by the fact that all staff have feelings of mutual co-operation and a knowledge that all can contribute. The firm itself is likely to be oriented towards quality of response and service and also to quality of product. To achieve these goals everybody recognizes that there must be high levels of communication and trust. The systems inaugurated by the firm must observably serve its people as well as the task and, as part of it, people will have adopted a mindset that seeks to produce excellence and innovation through co-operation rather than competition. Teamwork and mutual support will consequently be regarded as a priority by the organization and its staff, to the ultimate benefit of customers.

This is not an easy culture to achieve and it represents a considerable challenge to the firm's leadership to make it happen. Studies have shown that most individuals would value more mutuality within their cultures and consider that they are on the receiving end of too much transaction.

But which culture is the right culture to aim for if we accept that the emphasis should be on innovation as a key element of the overall strategy of most organizations? And should it be a part of an organization's strategy to steer its own culture to one that best helps it to meet the perceived needs of the marketplace?

The answer to the second question posed above must be a resounding 'yes' and we will examine the 'how to' of that in Chapter 7. However, the answer to the first question represents more of a dilemma. If we look back at both 3M and Oticon, then it is possible to see distinct elements of a self-expression approach within the former and high degrees of mutuality within the latter, albeit degrees of mutuality that are shaken up before the mutuality becomes clannish and any creative abrasion through diversity is lost. The answer must lie in achieving an uneasy balance between self-expression and mutuality.

Not all individuality is wrong and not all teamwork is productive; some people are capable of enormous achievement through their dedicated solo work, while at the same time teams have been shown time and time again to produce more than the total individual efforts of their members. So, if innovation often comes about as a result of flexible responses to the demands of the market, then it is up to the strategist to look closely at the needs of the organization's staff. It is imperative to recognize that different people are motivated by different things, and adjust both the personal approach as well as the many different entities that make up an organization's culture accordingly. While models of culture are a useful guide to what the organization could look like, it is up to you to decide exactly what will best fit your organization, or department, at a particular moment in time – and the best way of making that decision probably lies in asking your staff the right searching questions and then listening to the answers.

Finally, when experimenting with innovative processes or methods of operation, always be prepared for the unexpected. This especially was the case when one Tesco superstore decided to experiment with late night opening in the run up to Christmas. They were literally besieged by eager customers all night and had to postpone their original closing time several times in order to cater for the continuous influx of customers. In the end, the store management were forced to concede that the success of the experiment had exceeded all expectations and had placed their ability to manage that evening under severe pressure.

## Marketing – models and tools

One of the most fundamental strategic questions must be 'What is my organization's relative competitive position within the industry and how can I improve it?' This is the question that links the changing business environment, progress in technology and alterations in market demand to the levels of knowledge within your organization and its ability to exploit the knowledge via creative innovations. It is the key question that links the firm's internal world to the external world. It is the marketing question.

A number of strategic marketing models exist and many of them force us to think about applications, innovation and positioning. Marketing can be described as the commercial side of a firm's innovative progress. How do we let the world know what we have achieved? How do we get the world to buy it? If this sounds like advertising or brand management, then that is only part of the story. When you look for markets for your products and innovations the search itself may affect and change the whole direction of the organization. The process may lead you into new markets and out of old ones; it may change the way you operate and, in the long run, the whole character of the company.

Before looking at some of the marketing tools that underpin strategic decisions about where to apply effort, or where to stop applying effort, we need to look at another version of the key marketing question.

For any product there is a total sum of money that people will ultimately spend on it. If the product is luxury chocolates let us call it the chocolate pot. The size of the pot may be growing or it may be shrinking and just by virtue of being in that business we will have a certain share of that pot, or may desire a larger share. It is not, however, that simple; we will need to ask several searching questions in order to position ourselves most effectively in relation to that pot. For example:

- Is the pot growing or shrinking?
- Do we want to stay in that pot, or do we want to move into another?
- Are we happy with our share of the pot?
- Do we want a larger share or do we want to get out of that pot altogether?
- Do we have a new sort of chocolate that will have a major impact on the pot and on our share of it?

The following marketing models help us both to pose and answer key questions such as these.

## Boston Consulting Group growth–share matrix

Using this model of the marketplace requires you to analyse your product mix against the relative growth of the markets they compete in and the share your products have in them. Thus, in Figure 5.1 those products with a high share of a growing

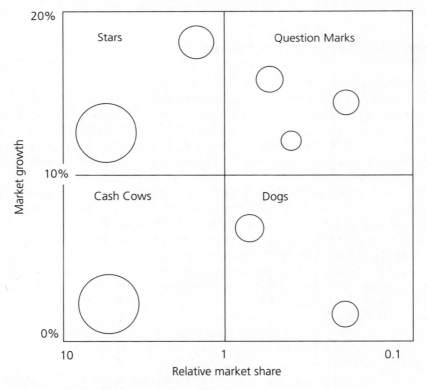

**Figure 5.1    Boston Consulting Group's growth–share matrix**

market are regarded as Stars, those with a high share of a static market are known as Cash Cows (to be milked for all they are worth while the going is good), those products that have a small share of static markets are Dogs and consequently good for nothing, while those products that have a small share of a growing market are the Question Marks and the key question then is: what must we do with them to increase their share?

The answer to that question must lie in the firm's ability to increase its attractiveness and differentiation through careful and timely innovations. Indeed, the question of innovation hangs over the fate of the Dogs, Cash Cows and Stars alike. Could innovations within that marketplace or to certain products change the desirability of a product or size of the marketplace itself?

## Ansoff's matrix

This illustration of the choices open to a firm was developed in 1968 (see Figure 5.2). In this matrix of the product options and market options available, the choices

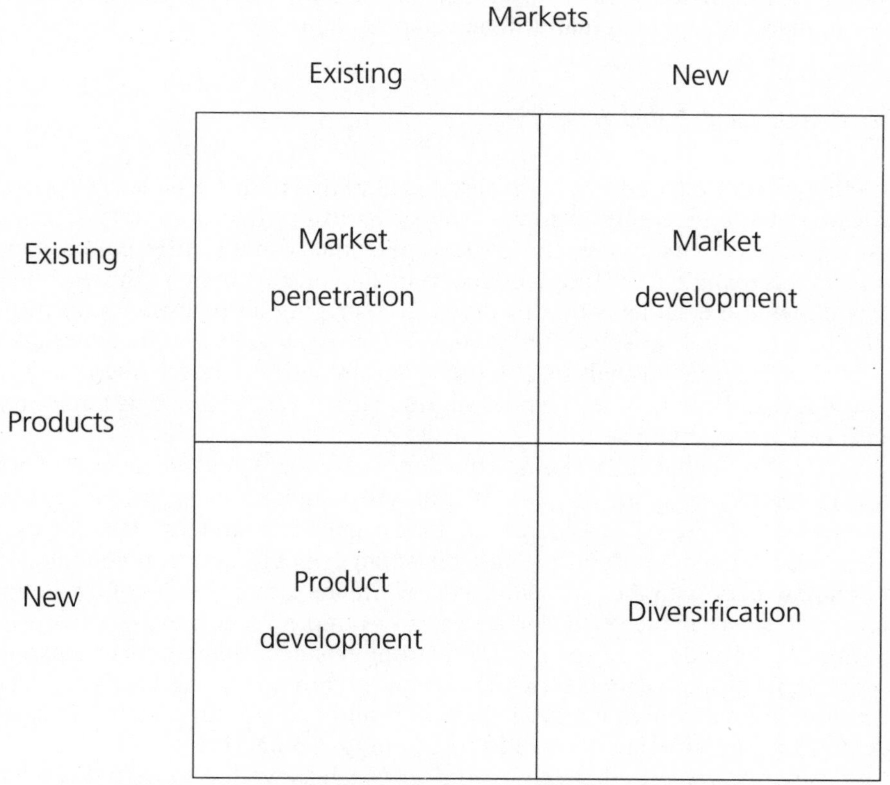

Markets

|  | Existing | New |
|---|---|---|
| **Existing**<br><br><br>**Products** | Market penetration | Market development |
| **New** | Product development | Diversification |

**Figure 5.2    Ansoff's matrix**

of expansion via new products in current markets and new products in new markets are starkly portrayed and the actions that a firm should take are illustrated. For example (keeping the chocolate pot firmly in mind), if you have an existing product and see a new market for it, you should do all you can to develop the market itself – you increase your product's potential sales by doing so. On the other hand, a new product will need a great deal of development and work to be done on and around it for it to be able to do well in an existing market.

Arguably, since Ansoff first drew up his model the need for firms to orientate their strategies to being more active in the lower half of the matrix has become more pressing. Gavin Barrett (1995) in *Forensic Marketing* uses the term new product development in place of innovation but places it as central to a firm's strategy:

> NPD is concerned to push out the frontiers of experience and discover markets that can be exploited profitably. For this reason alone NPD must be central to strategy. When coupled with a relentless drive to identify the fundamental characteristics of markets, that are likely to be sustained into the future, NPD is an ideal way to ensure that the organization remains responsive to markets, and imaginative in developing them.

## Multifactor portfolio analysis

This technique is often used by companies that have diversified products, or operating divisions who are trying to find a way of focusing their corporate strengths against the markets which have the greatest potential for their different products. Sometimes this technique is called product portfolio management as the method of analysis is much the same as that involved in managing an investment portfolio. Essentially, it is a tool for selecting the most effective strategy for the deployment of the firm's assets via the analysis of the varying strengths of the business, in terms of its products and services, against the varying attractiveness of the different markets into which they could be sold.

The range of potential strategies and the factors used as a guide to assessing both the market attractiveness and the particular business strength to be assessed against the market are illustrated in Figure 5.3. In the matrix, individual businesses or divisions are represented according to their strength in relation to potential competitors in the market on the horizontal axis, while the attractiveness of a potential market is portrayed on the vertical axis. So, for example, an aggressive expansionist approach is considered necessary for a strong business that wants to make the most of a highly attractive market, while a business with few strengths of product or approach in an unattractive market is basically into damage limitation – it would need to limit its investment in order to avoid putting itself at risk.

Of course, the strategies dictated by this approach as well as those indicated by the Ansoff and Boston grid approaches are fine in theory but fall into the same trap as much of micro-economics. They rely on a slavish expectation that logic should

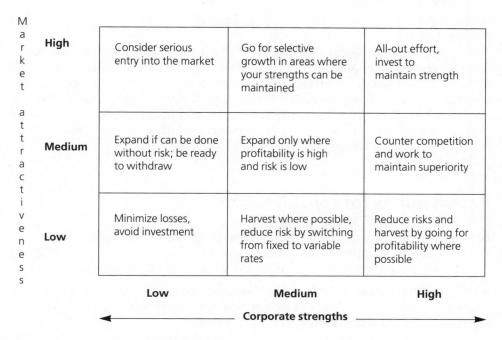

| | | Low | Medium | High |
|---|---|---|---|---|
| **M**arket attractiveness | **High** | Consider serious entry into the market | Go for selective growth in areas where your strengths can be maintained | All-out effort, invest to maintain strength |
| | **Medium** | Expand if can be done without risk; be ready to withdraw | Expand only where profitability is high and risk is low | Counter competition and work to maintain superiority |
| | **Low** | Minimize losses, avoid investment | Harvest where possible, reduce risk by switching from fixed to variable rates | Reduce risks and harvest by going for profitability where possible |

**Corporate strengths**

**Figure 5.3    Multifactor portfolio analysis**

reign supreme in fields where human beings make decisions on subjects involving other human beings. In stating that a firm will, of necessity, follow certain paths they take a totally logical, A-brained approach. In reality, decisions are often taken on a whim or perhaps because the chief executive has a pet product or favourite product range. Consequently, while these approaches act as a useful guide to strategic decision-making, do not expect to see their logic acted out in every strategy. And then many decisions are made on the basis of intuition and 'gut feeling'; paradoxically, these are quite often the best decisions!

# Conclusion

While all of the above strategic marketing tools have their place, the trouble with so much of the marketing carried out by marketing departments is that it is often so hidebound by statistics and procedures that the function in itself can lose its ability to think innovatively or to be fully aware of the many opportunities that are 'out there'. Marketing, of course, must be analytical but cannot afford to be too A-brained. The marketing models are useful but must not totally take the place of intuition or inventiveness. Above all, the marketing models must themselves be regularly scrutinized to see whether they remain Stars in themselves and that they are not slipping back towards becoming Dogs. For example, it is said that the

Internet will change everything – as pre-Internet models how will they stand up to the post-Internet age?

And when looking at the implications of the strategic decisions implied by the models, never forget the inevitable human consequences of those decisions. Perhaps the last word, therefore, should go to Henry Mintzberg (1996) who put together a number of tongue-in-cheek 'easy steps to destroying real value'. Here is my favourite: 'When in trouble, rationalize, fire and divest: when out of trouble expand, acquire and still fire (it keeps employees on their toes): above all, never create or invest anything, it takes too long.'

Sounds familiar!

## Action points for consideration

● Examine where innovation is really happening in the wider business scenario. How might this affect your business and what steps is your business taking either to keep abreast of it, or to take advantage of developments?

● Look at the opportunities that exist for innovation in the arena in which your organization does business. Have you and your organization stopped to ask the right questions when faced with various stimuli?

● Ask yourself whether your organization has taken steps to create a culture or environment in which innovation can flourish. If not, why not – and what can be done about it?

● Experiment by using a marketing tool such as the growth–share matrix to assess the ideal strategy for your organization. What is actually happening? What are the implications for both innovation and new product development?

# Chapter 6
# Strategy and change

As we surge towards the millennium and beyond, the most exciting view from today must be the view of tomorrow – the future.

Yet, as the world's politicians sharpen their verbal darts in order to denigrate each other's policies or belittle their achievements; as organizations invent intricate methods of measuring the quantity of work produced rather than the value it adds; as we continue to subject our precious planet to a slow death by pollution, ignoring the multiple warning signals it is giving us – it does appear that we have all fallen into the trap of looking around but not forward. It is a perennial truth that those who only concern themselves with today's issues will be continually surprised by tomorrow's. For those who fail to focus on the future, it is hard to feel much more than anger, pity or regret. Many of these ostriches will not reach it and those who do will be ill-prepared – they will have little or nothing to contribute to it.

All the time certainties, icons of what we have come to take for granted, come and go; others fade more slowly but then are suddenly seen no more. In 1997, Britain gave back one of her final colonies, Hong Kong, to China and at the handover ceremony, the Royal Yacht *Britannia* officiated at her last official cruise. Two icons disappeared at a stroke and at the 'party of all parties' after the handover, many Americans joined in the celebrations. However, did they stop to think about the changes that were rocking their own country – the fact that English, already the minority language in New York City, may soon be the minority language across the US? So, what new icons can be put in the place of the old? Can the future be made to look even better than when comfortable bastions of the disappearing past were still with us?

It is the individual leader, or the forward-thinking organization, that can put the strategies in place that will, in fact, provide answers to those and the hundreds of other questions that press us when we consider the future – and the changes that it must inevitably bring with it. It is the complex interweaving of these strategies that will allow us to substitute the threatening word 'change' with the more positive word 'progress'.

# Change – the headlong gallop

Change is inevitable and so much a part of our very existence that we cannot ignore it. To be fair, most do not ignore the changes that happen all around us and most of us will agree that change is taking place faster than ever before with the coming of the information age. True, but if you were to stop and consider that the arrival of the millennium will only celebrate a mere 730 000 days since the time of Christ and the start of the existing calendar, then the overall rate of progress has been quite staggering. So where *are* we now? An advertisement for Putnam Investments quipped, 'You think you understand the situation, but what you don't understand is that the situation just changed'. How true! And how do we differentiate the various elements that make up the cycle? For example, in Chapter 5 we examined innovation: where does it come into the picture? Innovation is without doubt part of the change process but change, as such, is independent of any innovations that may be taking place. Change is an inevitable consequence of the fact that we all live in an ever-changing universe and consequently two imperatives exist for the strategist:

1.  You must be ready for and anticipate change as part of your overall strategy – this must be part of your strategic mindset.

2.  You must be prepared to make change happen – to make the elements of change dance to your tune wherever possible. This can be done by promoting or embracing innovations but always remember: change itself is one of the key reasons why both strategies and strategists exist; change management and strategy formulation should be interdependent.

As the future rushes to meet us, the job of trying to predict it has reached something of a high art form. Hamish McRae (1994) has given us a fascinating series of provocations on the shape of the future which are based on a series of economic forecasts, and the whole field of systems thinking sets out to make predictions about the short-term future based upon the logical and cyclical interplay of cause and effect. But in the end, the future still has the ability to surprise us. For example, in the first decade of the twentieth century nearly 70 per cent of the UK's workers were in agriculture. How many farmers, or indeed industrialists, would have predicted at that time that the proportion would have sunk to 2 per cent by 1990 – or indeed that those working in production or manufacturing would have shrunk to 22 per cent and still be falling, while those working in data services would be heading towards 30 per cent of the workforce? This trend is, in fact, a global phenomenon. It has also been estimated that in the year 2000, no developed country will have more than 12 per cent to 15 per cent of its workforce in the traditional role of manufacturing goods. Service and knowledge management is already the most populated area of employment in the US with about 66 per cent of workers in this sector. No, the future does have the ability to surprise us and the theory of chaos is oddly seductive. But how do you, as a strategist, learn to thrive amidst all this change, irrespective of whether it is all a result of random chance or alternatively the product of logic and order?

A compelling answer to the above question might well be seen in a dry remark made by the CEO of Sony that 'The only way to be able to predict the future is to create it'. But that, of course, is easier said than done; not everybody succeeds. Perhaps this is because forging the future is difficult in itself – as well as the fact that as soon as you start, you are up against the ambitions and activities of other people who may also be seeking to mould it to their own individual ambitions. A study of world history shows us that only a few powerful individuals have been able to push forward towards their destinies, sweeping the weaker aside with Genghis Khan-like determination. The rest have needed a more cautious approach and to understand the processes, the elements of change, in order to give relevance to their strategies and, in fact, to make change work for them.

## Definitions and processes of change

We are all part of change, subject to it and, of course, continuously changing ourselves. In his 1970s best-seller *Future Shock*, Alvin Toffler (1973) argued that everything without exception is subject to change; some things may change more quickly than others but even supposedly unchanging things like stones and mountains react with their outside worlds and change. Not for nothing is the original metre-length rod locked away in an airtight safe and hardly ever brought out into the light of day!

But what exactly is change? Change could be defined as the 'process of making or becoming different'. However, in order to clarify these somewhat esoteric words, the definition itself needs to be broken down into its component parts:

- *Process*   This word implies that there will normally be a sequence of actions that make the change take place. Sometimes this sequence will be planned, sometimes what happens will appear much more haphazard.

- *Making*   Here a definite purpose is evident. If you want to improve the skills of your workforce, you will have to take certain actions that put new knowledge in their direction or which allow them to learn.

- *Becoming*   All things will become different over a period of time. That is inevitable. If, for example, you do not help your workforce to take on new skills or knowledge, things will not stay the same. Some will become de-motivated and leave, others will become less effective in many different ways and all will grow older; albeit not necessarily wiser.

- *Different*   This is the end result of the change process and, after an intervention, the 'difference' can take a number of alternative forms. For example, the organization or situation may have developed, it may be still in a situation of transition or it may have been totally transformed and its new state may bear little resemblance to the old.

We will return to the various types of differences later in this chapter, but suffice it to say here that most studies of organizations across the globe have indicated that the majority are in the middle of dramatic transformations! The reason? Everywhere there can be observed fundamental changes in markets, in consumer preferences and in the power balance of nations or economies. These in turn demand a parallel and perhaps disproportionate response in the mindsets and actions of organizations and industries.

A powerful example of this phenomenon can be seen in the battle for European TV ratings and advertising revenue between long-established US programme producers and new, aggressive European competitors. In the 1980s, European television was characterized by state-run monopolies that concentrated on showing cheap local productions or US re-runs. However, an energetic rebirth of sophisticated, high-budget European programmes is now drawing local audiences – and advertisers. For many years companies such as Time Warner, Sony-Columbia and Walt Disney assumed that US culture was eternally exportable. Now, faced with competition principally from the Germans, French and Italians, these organizations are staring down the gun barrel of indifference. *Business Week* (1997b) reported that 'since buying the English language Super Channel in 1993, NBC Inc has discovered that European viewers want more and more local fare. Although Super Channel reaches 60 million Europeans, "It doesn't get big enough audiences to even bother measuring," says Arnaud Dupont of Mediametrie, a French ratings agency.'

So, being big, being long-established, being powerful is really of no advantage in the no-holds-barred game of competition and change. One theory for the demise of the dinosaur was that a small insignificant animal appeared on the scene. It did not bother to confront the dinosaur head on – but its favourite meal was dinosaur eggs! So the whole concept of competition and change is one that is ripe for study, and while the mechanics of competition have been subjected to exhaustive examination, the same cannot truly be said of the processes of change, with the following exception.

## The Warwick studies

Some of the most powerful research on the process and management of change was carried out by the Warwick University Business School. This comprehensive study looked at the process of making change happen in organizations and divided it into four main areas, each of which was made up of a number of sub-features. We will overview these areas, along with some of their main messages for the strategist, before putting them into a more general model for making change happen effectively and sustaining the initiative.

The study looked at change from the following perspectives, each of which deserves some attention as they contain powerful advice to any strategist who is seeking to move the organization towards a shape or form that positions it better to meet the demands of the ever-evolving business environment.

## Getting started – energy and mobilization

There is a certain mathematical inevitability in the acceptance and implementation of change; it goes something like this. When the majority of people involved realize that the benefits of change outweigh the benefits of the *status quo* and also realize that change is possible, realizable and necessary – then it will happen. If these components do not complement each other, then change will either not happen, or only take place after a great deal of conflict and grief. The Warwick findings endorse this philosophy but go further by describing some of the actions that leaders and organizations have taken to make this formula work. Ever pragmatic, the findings offer sound advice both to those initiating change as well as those on the receiving end. As the findings are lengthy, I will only dwell on those aspects that are of most use to the strategist.

### Real and constructed crises

Even when change is critically necessary, it is often difficult to persuade people of the necessity for it. It is so easy to stay in the comfort zone of the *status quo*, the tried and tested. Statements like 'If it ain't broke, don't fix it' abide and nothing gets done. The key reason why people resist change in these circumstances is that they do not perceive the threat that not embracing change implies. Richard Adams in his classic story *Watership Down* summed up this complacent attitude with his description of the comfortable rabbits who would not leave their warren despite the fact that the hero perceived danger. The main problem was that the hero could not articulate the danger in a way that could shake the others out of their complacency, so the rabbits did not move – and were gassed by the farmer!

It is much the same in the world of work. We are all in danger of being too comfortable and so the danger needs to be clearly spelt out. Often a real and current crisis will mobilize people more effectively than some vague looming threat. The Warwick study found that where the crisis was real, people were shocked into action but it also cited examples where leaders had manufactured crises by producing 'fixed' sets of accounts that were so calamitous that people were stimulated into enthusiasm for change – anything to get out of the current situation.

Personally, I would not advocate this approach; leaders who lie to their people sacrifice one of the key components of good leadership – integrity. By doing so they start to ride the tiger! However, all leaders, all strategists worth their salt, should be able to scan the business scenario and be able to spell out the potential crises inherent in not changing. It is not difficult and the real passion communicated as an ingredient of integrity will serve to make that job easier. At Ikea, for example, CEO Anders Moberg, when appointed successor to Ingvar Kamparad, decided that, despite the organization's obvious success, what was working at present would probably not work in the future and in 1995 he warned employees that the organization was 'in crisis'. He explained, 'I wanted to wake the organization up' (*Business Week*, 1997c). The immediate results of this intervention were dramatic. Within two years the retail chain's sales had jumped 21 per cent despite the fact that many of its commodities were already priced some 20 to 30 per cent below those of its rivals.

### Leading change – champions and teams

Someone has to lead the change initiative on your behalf. Teams, with all they can contribute to creativity, all the benefits of support that membership can bring, can lend immense energy to any change initiative but the word I really want to focus on here is the word 'champion'.

A team may champion an initiative and can drive change forward through its actions as a focused project team, but in fact the essential element of the word 'champion' is that of ultimate responsibility for success. Consequently, it tends to be individualistic and, in a strategic context, rightly so. A champion is someone who speaks out for the project, who supports it, drives whatever actions are necessary for completion and who, in the end, takes the credit for success. Being a champion is not an easy role as your future career and success become integrally linked with the success of the change initiative in question. From a strategist's viewpoint, however, it is useful to appoint one or more champions to drive home the change; they will be committed and they will be focused on results. In the end, it is all about accountability.

### Broad visions, not blueprints

The Warwick study found that a broad vision of the future, communicated with passion and energy, tended to mobilize people towards the desired end. However, the vision needed to be stated in such a way that it gave plenty of leeway for action to those responsible for its implementation. Anything too prescriptive tended to curb creativity and above all else a sense of ownership, a sure recipe for disillusionment. Freedom to do one's own thing, to customize, innovate and adapt within the overall vision, was seen to be vital – especially when the organization needed to maintain commitment in the longer term.

At the same time, those responsible for communicating the initial vision needed to think carefully about the information flows in the organization. What are the right channels for communicating not just the vision but also the progress towards it? Should these channels be formal or should the grapevine be allowed to do its bit? On the other hand, if change is in the air, should new methods of communication be considered? As always, method and timing are essential.

### Using deviants and heretics

This is an old ploy often used by the politically astute. In any situation where change is pending, there will be the prophets, those who have not accepted the *status quo* for some time, those who advocate something new. The Warwick study found that organizations which used their deviants positively, by allowing them to speak out against the existing order before change was formally instigated, had paved the way forward in the most subtle way possible. The old order is undermined, thoughts about new processes or structures given an initial airing and the initiative is seen to come from within the organization rather than having been imposed on it. The whole situation contains a certain beautiful simplicity!

## The long haul – sustaining energy

Of course, once the change process has started, it is vital to maintain the commitment, energy and enthusiasm with which it was launched. This is not always easy as, for a start, not everyone will have accepted what is going on in the first place. Consequently, once the various actions or projects that constitute the change are under way, it is in many respects necessary to work even harder to maintain the momentum than it was to set the wheels in motion. The Warwick study pointed at the following pragmatic necessities.

### Consistent drive from the top
This is an absolute necessity but in fact does not happen as naturally as you might think. Very often the initiator of the original strategy is highly visionary but is so wedded to the idea of change, is so keen to continually explore new possibilities, that boring concepts such as the implementation of plans are of little interest. This high D-brain, low B-brain behaviour is not only maddening to other people but also has the effect of convincing them that those at the top are not seriously committed.

### Marrying top-down pressure and bottom-up concerns
While consistent drive from the top is necessary, the study found that when the flow was only one way, it tended to be self-defeating. There can have been few change situations where people have not felt some apprehension, where the passing of familiar customs or accepted hierarchies has not posed a threat, whether real or imaginary. Strategists who push for change without either considering or listening to the understandable fears of those affected by the changes are only letting *themselves* down. As the old adage goes, 'He who has ears, let him hear'.

At the same time, the sensitive change agent will appreciate that, in times of change, people need some form of sanctuary from the purposeful onslaught of the future. Consequently, the study recommended that those responsible maintained 'zones of comfort and relative continuity'. These could be departments or functions where the new practices or procedures were not yet implemented. In due course things would change there, but not yet. Somehow the (temporary) continuation of the old in the presence of the new gives great comfort and although this sounds illogical, in fact it may help to bed in the new.

### Finding the most creative approach to staff issues
In the end it is the people involved who will make or break any change initiative. If the people will not change, you will have to change the people and while some casualties are often inevitable, a large-scale loss or turnover of staff in reality means that you have failed. All too often change is associated with loss or sadness and when this is indeed the result of change all the old prejudices against it are borne out. So how do we get round this problem?

The Warwick study found that there were a number of ways in which energy and commitment could be maintained in the longer term. Among others these included refashioning the reward and recognition system. This may take time but the principle is simple and goes back to the oldest theory of motivation, that of stick and carrot. For example, if you require new behaviours of people, it makes sense to design salary or bonus systems that reward the new behaviours you want to see, and by the same token, do not reward the behaviours you do not wish to see. Once the new systems are fully in place it is then sensible to move from rewarding effort to rewarding performance.

Other successful tactics that the study noticed included finding and using role models. If a department or an individual had successfully adapted to the changes and was now performing well, then it made sense to publicize the fact and illustrate that these were the behaviours that were now required. This might mean that the overall knowledge and skill base of whole areas of the organization might need to be changed, with all that implied in terms of training or coaching. It also implied that some areas of the organization might be more receptive to change, or find it more easy to adapt to, than others. Consequently, different approaches or different levels of energy might be needed for different departments. Some areas would be less receptive than others and therefore would require more effort and, dare one say it, more tender loving care.

While the Warwick studies provide some useful insights into how organizations have managed internal change in order to meet changing external circumstances, they by no means cover the whole complex picture of change management. If one thing is indisputably true, it is the fact that change is constant, it is accelerating and that to successfully implement their strategies, organizations must constantly change and reinvent themselves. It is *how* they do this that can lead to make or break and, in the end, the *how* usually centres on the way that those caught up in the change – the people – are treated. This is a crucial factor in all change management initiatives and, although by no means ignored in the Warwick studies, from here on we shall move on to concentrate on this people factor and the insights into individual reactions to change that can make you a good or bad agent of change, and therefore by the same token a good or bad strategist.

## Change management – getting the timing and approach right

All too often those responsible for initiating change or even writing about it see it as something that is done to people rather than something that quite rightly might cause anxiety, or even fear. What a tragedy: if the history of the human race is really a history of change, must it be a history of fear rather than a history of progress? If change really does take place for the benefit of people (and if it does not, what on earth is the point?) is it not a tragedy that it is something that usually engenders at best suspicion and at worst downright fear? The answer lies within us as strategists and change agents; the impediment lies within us also. Tom Peters summed it up well in *Thriving on Chaos* (1987) when he said, 'Constant change programmes surely do threaten many people, especially traditional supervisors and middle managers. But constant change is thoroughly consistent with pursuing perfection in quality and service. Change must become the norm, not cause for alarm'. Sir John Harvey-Jones (1994) was also close to the point, albeit rather less understanding of the dilemmas facing those affected by change, when he said, 'Make the *status quo* more dangerous than the unknown.' This could well be interpreted as putting the poor victim of change between the proverbial rock and the hard place. Surely there are better ways – there have to be!

To be fair Harvey-Jones is not alone. There are many others who promote the absolute need for organizations to be flexible and adaptable to change. It is often portrayed as a stark choice – 'change or die' – and the truth is that if organizational mindsets fail to change at approximately the same rate as the external scenario, then eventually the gap will become too large; it will be unbridgeable and that probably will spell the end. A potent example here is that of IBM who refused to read the changes taking place in the world of computer design and applications until it was almost too late. This problem is illustrated in Figure 6.1. The challenge for the strategist is to work with this model in mind; it can never be an exact measure but can help prompt the timing, scale and method of interventions.

A wide variety of pundits have stressed the need for leaders and strategists to keep the pressure on the organization (in other words on the people within it) in times of change. Hamel and Prahalad (1993) coined the expression 'Strategy as stretch and leverage', a powerful design for a strategy that stated that true competitiveness could only be achieved by analysing a number of areas where the organization needed to stretch its people and resources vigorously in order to rise to new challenges. These areas of stretch could, they stated, be in anything from the conquering of new markets to changing the processes and methods by which they addressed them. All good fighting talk. But what about the people who are

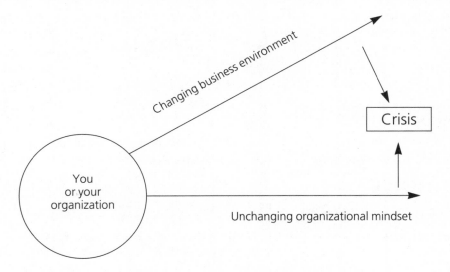

**Figure 6.1    Change management**

supposed to help the organization do the stretching, the people who are caught between the challenging unknown and the dangerous present? The people on whose good judgement, on whose commitment, goodwill and support a stretching change initiative may succeed or flounder? What do they need?

In addressing this question it is useful to look at the number of days lost due to stress every year. In the UK these amount to an amazing 320 million per annum and if we consider what these must add up to on a worldwide basis the figure must be staggering. An indication of where the stress of change can hit people is shown in Figure 6.2 where I have drawn up a Richter scale illustrating how various levels of stretch, or lack of it, can affect those involved.

In Figure 6.2, the effect of various levels of stimulation on the staff involved is portrayed. If there is no shake-up of vision and values, if no strategy is offered or one put forward that is not challenging or which does not present any real effort needed on the road to gaining it, then people are not stirred from their comfort zone. They may intellectually grasp the need to change but they are not jerked out of their existing mindsets or approaches. In short they are not sufficiently stimulated to do anything. They may be 'shaken – but not stirred!'.

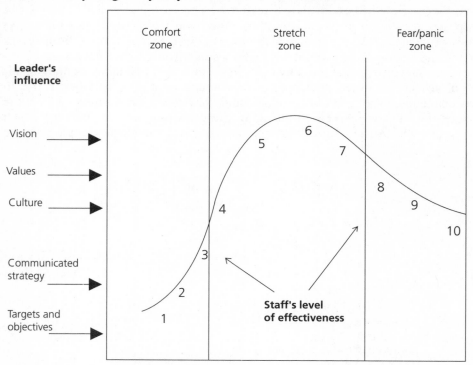

**Note:** It is best to maintain a certain level of 'stretch', without overdoing it as then staff become less effective.

**Figure 6.2     A Richter scale of stretch versus effectiveness**

On the other hand, if the stimuli are too great then people see the vision of the future and its accompanying strategy as a threat. Consequently, most of their efforts will be employed in trying to reduce the threat or in playing political games in order to ensure their own safety. The other common consequence is that people will simply do nothing as they feel over-challenged, trapped and threatened. In short, they will behave in much the same way as a rabbit trapped in the headlights of an oncoming car – frozen and immobilized as the threat bears down on them. As Edmund Burke said, 'No passion so effectively robs the mind of all its powers of acting and reasoning as fear.' So how do you ensure that people are motivated in the right way and to the right degree by the changes that lie ahead?

The answer must lie in hitting the right note – in achieving the correct balance between challenge and empathy, between communicating the vision and showing an understanding of its impact. It lies in finding the balance between a communicated strategy that stirs collective ambitions and one that clearly shows people what lies ahead, what's in it for them personally and what achievable actions they can take in order to help make it happen. If the message comes across with the right balance of challenge, understanding and support, then it is most likely to bring about what is required to achieve the strategic objectives – namely commitment, enthusiasm, understanding and intelligent action.

A useful expression has crept into common usage, 'change weariness'. In 1997, at the International Competency Conference, Murray Dalziel, former Chief Executive of Hay/Mcber, told delegates that flexible, decentralized and fully empowered organizations would be unlikely to make the best use of their own collective knowledge and that 'highly disciplined processes' backed up by 'discipline, tight systems and even authoritarianism' were the best route to mobilizing a company's knowledge. I suspect that this sort of approach might mobilize something, although I doubt that it would be the organization's knowledge base, as this seems to go against all the acknowledged wisdom of ownership and commitment. Any changes that these hard-line tactics were to bring about would be no more than surface deep, steeped in change weariness and, like the proverbial house built on sand, destined to tumble down at the slightest provocation!

Change weariness seems to be a common complaint and the first step to finding a cure lies in asking what people actually need in times of change. The following section lists a few of the basic essentials. Like most items of plain common sense, they stem from someone having taken the time to ask the right questions.

# What people need in order to be committed in times of change

### 1. A chance to mourn the past

People will let go but, as in the case of saying goodbye to a loved one, there may need to be a wake, a chance to celebrate the old for the contribution it used to make and the good times it provided. If something has lasted for a number of years it is unlikely to have been wholly bad, even if it has outlived its usefulness. Acknowledge this human need and allow people to 'let go' properly and with dignity (even if with dignity means an evening at a bar or pub!); this acknowledgement of a human need will pay dividends out of all proportion to the initial investment.

## 2. Maximum advanced notice

People need time to prepare, they need time to make the mental jumps from the initial shock of hearing about the change, through the common phase of denial and then through to acceptance of it and eventual integration of it into their own behaviour.

## 3. Gradual integration of the new with the old

If this is possible it is a wise policy. Allow those involved in making the change work to run both systems together for a time. They will soon see the advantages of the new and abandon the old voluntarily.

## 4. Involvement at the planning and review meetings

This may seem obvious but it does not always happen. The devil lies in the detail and those involved in making the changes work often stare the detail, as well as the devil, straight in the face. Their views, their pragmatic experiences, can give the essential gloss of practicality to the most fanciful strategic plan.

## 5. The right management style

Be patient, tolerant but also firm. Achieving the correct balance between direction and support, between telling and listening, may be old hat in terms of management theory, but it works.

## 6. Teams that can carry the initiative

An enormous amount of research has shown that teams can be both more productive and creative than the solo efforts of a single individual. They have the added advantage of providing support for their members in times of change and uncertainty. Wherever possible let teams be responsible for both initiation and implementation.

## 7. Knowledge of progress and communication

All too often once a change has been initiated it is forgotten by senior management as new and exciting possibilities present themselves. However, strategic changes need to work in the long run and so results, achievements and progress need to be communicated regularly in order to inspire staff and ensure that they both see and share in the benefits.

### 8. Visible leadership

Few things are more de-motivating than the concept of the faceless planner, the unseen strategist or the light-footed leader who causes something to happen and then is seen no more. The generals of the First World War are still being pilloried for administering their disastrous strategies from 10 miles behind the trenches and do not bear comparison with the mobile, visible general, on both sides, in the Second World War. Be visible, be interested and above all be around. Be there, or beware!

So, there are a number of needs to keep in mind, and knowing them can make all the difference between change that lasts and contributes towards the overall strategic direction, and a change that peters out or is frustrated by opposition, lack of commitment or even sabotage. But it is possible to take the principles of good change management one stage further by examining ideas that can help you add an extra vital ingredient to the change initiative – the dimension of meaning.

# Finetuning the change – communication to overcome fear and resistance

Without meaning, in other words if people do not understand the purpose and reason for forthcoming changes, if they are not able to detect logic or reason in the unfolding strategies, then there will be a number of different possible negative reactions to any change initiative. These reactions may range from confusion to scepticism and from anxiety to downright fear. In fact, I consider that fear often plays such a common but negative role in organizational life that it is amazing that it is not discussed more frequently; perhaps people are afraid to do so!

There have been a few studies of the subject of fear in the US, although J. Gerald Suarez (1994), Director of Presidential Quality Management at the White House, successfully extended the work of Deming, that early 'guru' who managed to put a human face to the concept of quality management, in advocating the elimination of fear in the workplace so that employees were better able to work towards the fulfilment of the organization's strategy. I have used some of Suarez's valuable thoughts in this field as the basis of the organizational fear scan (see Figure 6.3). The questionnaire can be completed using either the organization as a whole as the main subject, or your own impact within it as the focus.

Simply answer yes or no to each question

1. Has your organization published a statement of core purpose, values, vision and guiding strategy?
2. Have concrete steps been taken to ensure that the statement is understood?
3. Do people accept that the targets implied in the statement are realistic and achievable?
4. Has the organization conducted an assessment to identify attitudes and barriers that inhibit performance?
5. If yes, has anybody taken action on the results?
6. Do you know what really worries people in the organization?
7. Do your peers or subordinates fear you?
8. Does your boss perpetuate fear?
9. Does a valid 360° feedback instrument exist in the organization?
10. Do you consider that people in your organization are having to do things against their better judgement?
11. Do you believe your subordinates trust you?
12. Do you trust your suppliers?
13. Do you trust your customers?
14. Do you trust the top management or your own boss?
15. Do you frequently ask for feedback?
16. Do you listen and act on it when feedback comes?
17. Do you tend to 'shoot the messenger' when bad news arrives?
18. Do you consider that your staff have all the information needed to carry out their jobs effectively and with understanding?
19. Do your staff have a say in selecting the means and processes by which their work is measured?
20. Have you taken all reasonable steps to ensure that your peers and staff acquire new knowledge and develop new skills?
21. Do you inform your staff of opportunities for individual advancement and development?
22. Do rumours abound in the organization?

**Scoring**

| Question | Yes | No |
|---|---|---|
| 1 | +3 | −4 |
| 2 | +1 | 0 |
| 3 | +2 | −2 |
| 4 | +2 | 0 |
| 5 | +2 | −3 |
| 6 | +2 | −1 |
| 7 | −2 | +1 |
| 8 | −2 | +1 |
| 9 | +2 | −1 |
| 10 | −3 | +3 |
| 11 | +1 | −2 |
| 12 | +1 | 0 |
| 13 | +1 | 0 |
| 14 | +2 | −2 |
| 15 | +3 | −3 |
| 16 | +2 | −3 |
| 17 | −3 | +3 |

**Figure 6.3**    **The organizational fear scan** (*continues*)

| 18 | +1 | −3 |
| 19 | +2 | −2 |
| 20 | +2 | −3 |
| 21 | +2 | −1 |
| 22 | −1 | +2 |

**To score**

Add up the total of your positive scores (+) and subtract this sum from the total of your negative (−) scores.

Range is +40 to −40.

**Analysis**

- Between +40 and +30. Excellent. Or are you deluding yourself?
- Between +30 and +20. Congratulations. Keep up the good work, can you do more?
- Between +20 and 0. Neutral. Could do better.
- Between 0 and −10. Your organization may be affected by creeping paranoia.
- −10 to −20. The atmosphere at work may be having a serious effect on effectiveness.
- −20 to −30. Fear is rife and trust is low.
- −30 to −40. Are you serious? Your organization probably resembles the KGB!

**Figure 6.3**     **The organizational fear scan** (*continued*)

# Moving on

Although the fear scan in Figure 6.3 is not a scientific instrument and the scores can only be taken as a somewhat light-hearted measure, it does hopefully provide food for thought. After all, if you have decided that fear is rife within your organization, to what extent are your attitudes and behaviour part of the problem? In looking at your answers to the questions, can you see where the solutions may lie? What are the answers and what are the antidotes?

The key to answering these questions lies in the way in which both the challenges of the future objectives as well as the changes that will be necessary to achieve them are described or portrayed. One method of ensuring that the challenges of the strategy are motivational rather than fear-inducing is 'leapfrogism'. This may sound weird but in fact it is simple common sense. When a stretching target, a BHAG (big hairy audacious goal), is identified it may sound intimidating. However, if that target can be broken down into a number of realistic steps, starting with the most immediate and achievable, then the ultimate goal will not seem so awe-inspiring. There is a process to follow and it goes like this:

1. Clearly state the stretching target. What is it? How will we know when we have reached it?
2. Identify what needs to have been achieved immediately before the target is reached. What does that involve in terms of actions and accomplishments?
3. Identify what needs to be in place in order to make those achievements happen.
4. Identify what needs to happen before that happens.

... and so on. In the end, you will find that you are faced with a number of sensible actions that are in themselves not hard to achieve. Both the plan and the process are now in place and under way.

An example of leapfrogism in action can be seen in the challenge that John F. Kennedy gave to the American people in that they would place a man on the moon by the end of the 1960s. This was a stretching target indeed given the existing state of technology at that time. However, when the task was broken down into its component milestones it became more realistic. The accomplishments necessary before landing someone on the moon were to develop technology that would enable blast off back to earth. What was necessary to achieve that? Before that it would be necessary to develop spacecraft capable of the total journey. What would need to be in place to achieve that goal? In the end the process boiled down to that of recruiting the right scientists and giving them the tools to do the job. What was needed for that? Money!

So that particular complex task could be broken down into a number of far more reachable objectives. The task of recruiting the right brains for the job and of finding the considerable sum of money to launch the process may have been a tough one but it was a lot less tough than the overall objective of landing a man on the moon. Of course, once the overall series of lesser objectives has been established, it is then necessary to sequence them from present to future in order to see whether they still make sense. And of course, the objectives may well change as the plan rolls out. But if the reason for the changes are made clear to all, that in itself should not be a problem. The process of leapfrogism is illustrated in Figure 6.4. When applied to less stretching strategic objectives than a moon-shot, it takes on an even greater power.

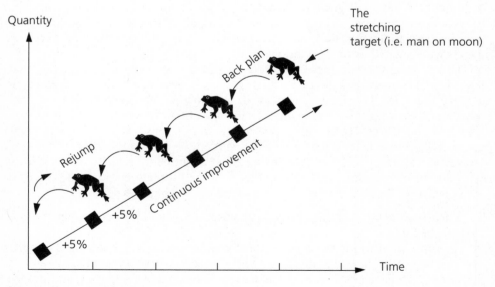

**Figure 6.4       'Leapfrogism'**

# Describing the changes

People are far more ready to accept change, more importantly to work towards it with energy and commitment, if they understand the nature of the change as well as the purpose behind it. They are also more likely to accept the changes that are happening all around them if they can accept that changes are inevitable, continuous and inescapable. Put this acceptance together with the realization that those at the top (the leaders, the strategists) understand the situation as well as how the staff feel about what is happening, and acceptance will become action as well as motivation. In other words, as already stated, if you simply engage people's heads you may get intellectual acceptance of the situation, but if you engage their hearts as well then you are more likely to stimulate the hands and feet – activity will happen.

Another model of change management is the 'freeze–unfreeze–re-freeze' model. The principle here is that methods, attitudes and processes will have been set (frozen) in a certain way and it is therefore the change agent's duty to unfreeze them (stir them up, deal with opposition, etc.) before re-freezing everything along the new desired lines. Unfortunately, as an approach, this does not work. If everything is in a state of continuous change then it cannot be re-frozen even if some new processes can be bedded in for a while. In my own organization, after we had all been given new computers and trained in their use, a senior person remarked to the computer consultants, 'Well, that's that then.' 'Just for the time being' came the cautious reply. Better by far to think in terms of what *sort* of change the organization is in fact facing and to orientate one's approach around that.

Organizational change can be broken down into three clear types:

1.  *Developmental*   This is the sort of change that simply builds on and improves on what already exists. It may streamline procedures, shorten response times, improve quality but at the end of the initiative things are not radically different.

2.  *Transitional*   Here the organization will be moving from one state to another. It may be changing its product base or introducing new technologies. It may well still be exploring where to go and what its final state of being may be.

3.  *Transformational*   Here the organization will be changing to a completely different state of being. The move may be from a manufacturing-based organization that has long prided itself on the excellence of its product quality to an organization that now accepts that excellence of quality is taken for granted and that the key differentiator in the future will be quality of service. Or the move may be from being a non-commercial wing of a civil service function to a function that now has to survive in the cut and thrust world of full commercial competition. It is interesting to note that most recent studies have shown that transformational change is easily the most prevalent. In other words, major strategic initiatives are being enacted in every theatre of work.

It makes sense that if you want people to react in a way that is consistent with the demands of the change situation, it will be necessary to describe the nature of the change accurately and to reflect this accuracy in the words you use. For example, if the change is developmental, it is better to use language such as 'We must adjust' or 'Develop what we have got' or 'We must get smarter at . . .' In other words the paradigm remains unaltered. When, on the other hand, the change is transitional in nature that sort of language will not suffice; instead words such as 'Explore new ways, leave the old behind, move on' are much more appropriate – the paradigm is being bent, if not broken. (See R. J. Marshak, 1993.)

When the change is transformational, the role of the change agent, or strategist, becomes much more one of the challenger and visionary. Here the words used must help others to recognize that the mould has been broken. Phrases such as 'Breaking with the past' or 'The past is dead' or 'Escaping from the strictures of the old' or 'Moving into the light of the new' all now describe what is happening in both the internal and external worlds. If, for example, the organization is reinventing itself as a service leader and recognizes that this entails a major move in the style of operating and thinking of its people, from being principally left-brained with a focus on analysis, technology and processes to a new paradigm of whole-brained thinking – a state where dealing with the customer, motivating one's own staff, and joint exploration of future possibilities with existing and potential clients are now equal priorities – it is not appropriate to use expressions like 'We must adjust'; they are simply not powerful enough. The language must match the situation and the resultant clarity should educate and liberate all concerned.

So, with change, as with many things in both business as well as other walks of life, the difference between success and failure depends upon a very human factor; quality of communication.

## Conclusion

Change has always been with us, always will be with us and will not go away. Change is both the parent of and the child of strategy; it is how you deal with it that counts.

Strategist, change agent, leader – it becomes difficult to separate the three. However, there are crucial differences. Differences not so much in the nature of the desired goals as in how they are achieved. In a recent series of interviews with a varied selection of leaders, I found that they all had one thing in common; they had a positive attitude towards change. This did not mean to say that they charged blindly towards it but that they tended to look to the possibilities that the future provided with a positive attitude. It is the behaviour of the leader that will make the difference between successful strategies or failed initiatives and in the end leadership is what leaders *do*. They can be good leaders or bad, effective change agents or purveyors of chaos, they can be strategic or unstrategic. In Chapter 7, we will look at the key components of strategic leadership and what they may mean for you.

# Action points for consideration

- Examine your own attitude towards change. Do you see it as a threat, an opportunity or as a stimulus for action?

- Change can be stretching for those involved. Examine the extent to which either you or your organization are getting the right balance between comfort, stretch or support for those involved.

- Analyse the extent to which fear may be rife within your organization. If levels are high, what can be done to alleviate it?

- Check that processes are in place to ensure that change is implemented consistently through 'to the end'. Avoid moving on to the next fad – sadism via faddism – nothing drives other people crazy faster than faddism!

- Look at the type of change that is going on around you. What implications are there for both strategic development and also for adopting the right sort of leadership style?

# Chapter 7

# The strategic leader

The various methods of and approaches to strategic analysis are but the servants of the organization. They have no purpose other than to help determine its present state of health, its future direction and the methods by which the goals incorporated within that direction are to be reached. Indeed, it has been claimed that the arrival of the Internet, with the huge influx of information it makes available, has made all the tools of strategic analysis redundant. While I do not subscribe to that particular theory, believing that the tools will now depend even more on the skills of the user, I do believe that the enormous amount of information available to us all will place greater demands upon the strategic leader.

The strategic leader, in contrast, is in turn master, servant and a member of the organization. This person could be regarded as both custodian and user of the tools; the stimulus for change and the person who makes it happen. However, is strategic leadership solely the province of the man or woman at the top of the organization? Is it just something done by boards under the title of corporate governance? Or can it be something that is part of the duties of those at other levels within that organization? My own view is that we have all got responsibilities to be strategic; this can be done both by assisting the CEO in the crucial task of defining the overall strategy and also by thinking strategically about those parts of the organization that fall within our own province. This may cause you to define a strategy that may well be independent of the overall strategy but which still reflects the core purpose of the organization and which contributes towards the final aims of the governing strategy.

Max Pree, CEO of Herman Miller, put the answer to the dilemma into focus when he said, 'The first responsibility of a leader is to define reality. The last is to say thank you. In between, the leader is a servant'. These wise words aptly put the responsibility for achieving strategic goals and for formulating strategies at all levels of empowered organizations.

But what are the skills of the strategic leader? How do they differ from those of non-strategic leaders and is it possible to be a leader without being strategic? Is the very idea of the non-strategic leader a 'no brainer'? In order to answer these questions it is necessary to examine the way that thinking about the very nature of leadership has developed over the years.

# Leadership theory – four stages of development

The concept of leadership only really came to be studied in the twentieth century and the studies have tended to fall into four groups of thinking, each of which has contributed to the overall body of knowledge about the subject by raising fundamental questions that other theories have either built on or disproved. In examining these four chronological generations of thought, I have paraphrased and omitted the ideas of many theorists. However, my intention is not to spell out a lengthy history of leadership theory, rather it is to help define the concept of strategic leadership by comparing the development of thinking about this elusive concept to the demands of the era in which it found itself – and out of this, identifying two separate but necessary forms of leadership: transactional and transformational leadership.

## Trait theory

This was an approach to thinking about leadership that was popular up until the 1940s. Its basic premise was simple. Leaders were considered to be born not made so, by implication, if you were not deemed lucky enough to have been born a leader, forget it! In the 1930s studies were initiated in the US to define what the traits of these born leaders were. In other words, the argument ran, if we can look at a number of people who are at the top of industry, commerce or the armed forces and see what they have in common, then we will have an excellent identikit picture of 'the born leader'.

Fortunately, the studies to prove this flawed idea failed at the first hurdle. The only common factor identified for these leaders was that they were all tall! No doubt, in looking at a cross-section of the richer and more privileged members of society, the studies identified those who had the benefits of better diets rather than radically superior leadership abilities. At the same time, it was only necessary to look back into history and see the number of short leaders such as Napoleon who would quickly show up these conclusions for the falsehoods that they in fact were.

## Behavioural theories

This line of thinking started in the 1940s and was popular into the 1960s. In fact, much of what was developed at this time still holds true; even if subsequent academics have refined and improved upon the arguments.

The essential idea here was that leadership can be taught and that good leadership is a matter of adopting the right sort of behaviour when attempting to lead other people. Paradoxically, it was the sudden entry of the US into the Second World War that did much to precipitate this line of thinking. After Pearl Harbor, the US needed to train up a large number of officers and senior NCOs in a hurry. Instructors at West Point Military Academy found that many who were sent to them for officer training, despite being from non-patrician families (and probably short as well!), did far better in training than more conventional officer material. So, leadership, it was decided, could be taught – but when peace resumed, another question then arose: 'Is there an ideal type of leader, and if so what makes that person ideal?'

A number of academics set out to answer that question and in doing so looked at the way that effective leaders set out to get other people to carry out tasks for them. Blake and Mouton (1994) were the most successful here and devised a grid by which it was possible to identify a leader's overall behaviour against the two criteria of emphasis placed on task and emphasis placed on relationships. The ideal leader, they stated, was a 9.9 – someone who scored high on task focus and high on relationships. For several years many aspiring leaders sought to be 9.9 leaders and in doing so ignored the fact that high task and high relationship emphasis, while being useful in many situations, was not relevant for all the complicated and demanding contingencies that a leader was likely to face. Something more flexible was called for!

## Contingency theories

These concepts, which were the descendants of the behavioural theories, first took root in the 1960s and still stand today as a useful guide to effective leadership. The core belief behind all such thinking is that 'There is no one best way to lead'.This was most loudly proclaimed by Hersey and Blanchard (1977) and then by Dr Kenneth Blanchard (Blanchard and Johnson, 1983) in the well-known theory of situational leadership.

The thinking behind situational leadership is simple but powerful. In short, it states that the most effective outcomes for a leader come when the leader adjusts his or her behaviour to meet the demands of the situation and the ability of his or her staff to deal with it. Hersey and Blanchard identified four main types of leadership behaviour based on the degree to which the leader mixed both directive and supportive behaviour in his or her approach. The behaviours were summarized as: directive, coaching, supporting and delegating. The key to success lay in matching the behaviour to the needs of the situation and in remaining flexible in approach in order to be effective. In other words, the relationship between leader and followers was seen as a transaction; the leader wants effort from the followers and needs to give them the right sort of leadership in order to release that effort. The concept of transactional leadership remains valid but it essentially describes transactions aimed at reaching short-term targets. The target may well be part of a strategy, but the process of enabling your staff to reach it is not in itself strategic.

At about this time, other writers such as Warren Bennis (1989) and John Kotter (1990) advanced the overall level of knowledge about leadership and Kotter especially made useful distinctions between leadership and management. It was their work that most clearly set the scene for the fourth stage of leadership thinking, a subject to which they continue to contribute.

## Transformational leadership

Here the idea of the leader as change agent takes over. The focus of thinking, while not disagreeing with the idea of transactional leadership, now points towards a series of more sophisticated demands that are increasingly being made on leaders. As we approach the millennium and the overall level of uncertainty in the world increases, as old truisms go out of the window and few new certainties take their place, as the planet shrinks and we increasingly talk about the global economy, life at work becomes more demanding for everybody; as do the expectations made of leaders at all levels. These expectations can be listed as follows:

- Changing organizations and the systems within them.
- Empowering others and working increasingly with and through self-managing teams.
- Changing people's mindsets.
- Managing meaning, and by doing so giving clarity of direction and purpose to others.
- Driving the strategy.

So, does the above list of somewhat obscure concepts fully define strategic leadership? Is that all there is to it? The answer to those questions is both yes and no. The role of the strategic leader most certainly is to transform both the organization and the mindsets of the people within it in order to enable it to meet the challenges of the future. But on the other hand, the list in itself is inadequate – what is it that the leader *must do* to be fully and effectively strategic? What are the key actions, attitudes and approaches of the leader that will enable change to take place and strategies to be successfully pursued?

# Being strategic – the maturation of leadership

In an earlier book on leadership (van Maurik, 1994), I defined three stages of development of leadership skills. These were *birth*, which involves understanding oneself and being able to use that self-knowledge, *growth,* which was all about understanding other people and being able to work with them, whether individually or in teams, and finally *maturation,* which was about having a vision, being able to persuade or inspire others, being able to manage change and also to develop and implement strategies. The essential point I was trying to make was that all the skills that you needed to develop as a leader had to be maintained throughout your time as a leader. So, when the focus of your job now meant that most of your time was spent defining and implementing strategies, it was more important than ever to retain a high level of self-awareness and a keen understanding of other people. To abandon these essentials meant that you were embarking on the fourth stage of leadership development – *decline*!

Consequently, it is necessary to define the overall essentials, or competencies, of good leadership before examining in greater detail the essential qualities of the effective strategic leader. The following list of competencies is a development of one that I used to test a variety of leaders in order to examine the nature of modern leadership. The competencies are developed from a mnemonic I devised to describe what I considered to be the essential qualities, or talents, of leadership. This was WIST and the letters stood for *W*isdom, *I*ntegrity, *S*ensitivity and *T*enacity. The main behavioural elements of WIST are reproduced below and expressed in terms of the competencies that constitute them. I have added a small number of competencies to reflect the increased emphasis here on strategy; otherwise the list is unchanged.

## Wisdom

- Able to create visions of the future, and pursue them.
- Intuitive, yet wise in the way the vision is pursued.
- Judges people and situations well.
- Has thoughts and opinions on the future of business methods and the nature of work.
- Inspiring when necessary. Capable of being a mentor at all times.
- Adept at influencing and persuading others.
- Able to see the big picture and to recognize trends.
- Capable of dealing with organizational politics – a communicator and networker.

## Integrity

- Demonstrates to others that they are worthy of trust.
- Does not operate on hidden agendas.
- Is open and honest in dealing with others.
- Does not shrink from candour when necessary.
- Able to give bad news.

## Sensitive (in approach)

- Can operate as a coach.
- Good listener.
- Able to empower and develop others.
- Understands the power of teams and how to work with them.
- Understands the constituents of good process and how to achieve it.
- Capable of continuous learning.
- A facilitator of learning and of situations.
- Looks for future opportunities in everything that happens.
- Looks for opportunities to motivate others.

## Sensitive (in thinking)

- Conforming in approach when necessary but capable of non-conformity.
- Able to challenge the conventional wisdom of situations, to bust paradigms.
- Able to handle diversity of approach and opinion.
- Understands that different things motivate different people; applies this understanding.
- Creative; can think outside the box.
- Able to think strategically and to communicate the strategies.
- Familiar with a number of strategic tools.
- A risk-taker when necessary. Adventurous and courageous.

## Tenacity

- Dynamic, energetic.
- Hard-working yet able to balance home and work life.
- Capable of handling own stress as well as that of other people.
- Disciplined in approach. Able to handle failure and setbacks.
- Tenacious – doesn't give up.
- Understands and copes with the pressures of power.
- Able to handle uncertainty and to help others to do so.
- Demonstrates optimism.
- Handles change well. Plans it and makes it happen.

So, from this list, what are the essential competencies or talents of a strategic leader? What skills must you develop, maintain and above all use? The list in itself is holistic; in other words it calls on a wide range of talents and for the leader to be able to operate effectively in all four quadrants of the brain. However, when thinking about strategy we need to select and focus on the essential few talents that will drive the organization forward.

I believe that the ability to be strategic is the defining hallmark of a mature and senior leader. Many leaders may stop at the transactional level in terms of their own development as leaders and may perform very effectively there. In fact, they may be deemed to have reached their final stage of maturity. However, while the ability to be an effective transactional leader is necessary at all times, it is not enough if your task is to move an organization forward to meet the needs of an ever-changing world – in other words to drive a strategy and to transform the organization in order to enable it to deliver that strategy. Here a different set of skills or competencies are required and these are listed below:

- To cope with the uncertainty of modern times and to forge an overarching direction for the organization.
- To devise and communicate a clearly defined vision.
- To influence the culture of the organization and move it towards one of continuous learning, adaptation, flexibility, and responsiveness.

- To create high levels of trust, responsiveness and motivation within the organization. To inspire where necessary.
- To be able to persuade and influence other people.
- To drive forward appropriate strategies based on sound evaluation of both the current situation and the future desired state.

We now need to examine these skills in order to illustrate what it is that you must think or do in order to earn the title of 'strategic leader'. Some of the skills have already been dealt with in earlier chapters and the fact that this has been necessary just serves to illustrate the fact that the skills of strategic leadership cannot be separated from the essential steps of strategy formulation and implementation.

## Exercising the skills

So what is it that good leaders make? In short, they make change happen, they make money for all stakeholders in the organization ranging from shareholders to the most junior worker, they make things happen and to do this they make a difference. These talents, especially the final two, can be regarded as the hallmarks of great leadership, whether we are looking at the commercial, political or religious arenas. And the essential competencies of transformational leadership illustrated above can be summarized in these few short phrases.

Within a challenging and often uncertain environment, the strategic leader must perform a variety of tasks to ensure that the organization moves ahead successfully. These tasks usually have one thing in common; they focus the effort and energies of those involved – first to interpret what is going on 'out there' and then to organize their efforts and activities in a way that will lead to success.

It is now necessary to go through the main talents involved here in order to extract the cusp of talents and actions implied.

### Forging direction out of uncertainty

In Chapter 2 we looked at the need for analysis as the initial step in strategic thinking and the discipline involved is essential when dealing with the increasing range of uncertainties thrown at us by modern times. But the process actually starts from within. When faced by the fact that so many old certainties have been thrown out of the window, it is necessary to deal with the resulting mental disequilibrium by throwing many of one's old beliefs, prejudices and mindsets out of the same window. To do anything else is dangerous and likely to leave you the victim of the dilemmas of change rather than their master. In a recent TV film on fox hunting the Master of a well-known fox hunt was interviewed concerning his feelings about potential legislation to ban the sport. He stated, 'First we lost the Empire, then the Church went to pot and now we are about to lose the countryside!' My reaction was initially of contempt and then of pity – here was somebody lost in a romanticized version of the past and unable to see anything positive in the possibilities of the future. This was an individual who was unable to conceive a vision that could take him beyond his own backdated paradigms. Perhaps he needed a short sharp shock to his conception of reality. What, for instance, would people of the old Empire have wanted? What of the thousands of women who desperately need to express their faith by taking holy orders?

This myopia of vision was aptly described by A. Bloom (1987) in *The Closing of the American Mind*:

> Freedom of the mind requires not only or not even especially the absence of legal restraints but the presence of alternative thoughts. The most successful tyranny is not the one that uses force to assure uniformity, but the one that removes the awareness of other possibilities, that makes it inconceivable that other ways are viable, that removes the sense that there is an outside.

It is all too easy to fall into restrictive, short-sighted patterns of thinking. However, by deliberately attempting to think creatively, by encouraging these thought processes in other people, it is possible to think one's way out of and through uncertainty. And from these paradigm-busting thought processes can spring the liberating vision – the vehicle that can help us conceptualize the future and set the direction for it.

This liberating process can be broken down into its component parts:

1.  First there must be desire. Strategy is born out of will. A will and desire for something different. At this stage it is not necessary to understand why you want something different; only to acknowledge that desire and to accept that you want change.

2.  Out of this desire must come reflection, dreaming and analysis. It is all too easy at this stage to be driven by the urgency of one's desire and to charge ahead. Therein lies failure. From the reflection must stem analysis of both self and situation ('Why do I want something different? In reality what is wrong? Why do I feel puzzled? What could the future look like?')

3.  From the analysis will emerge perspective. A first level of understanding of the situation. 'I start to see the situation from a variety of angles', 'I begin to sense what is wrong'. Or, 'I now start to see the way ahead, or what must be done'. And from the perspective must come resolution, the determination to do something, to make a difference. The quintessential urge that underpins both leadership and strategy.

4.  The affirmation of the desire should in turn stimulate decisions about future actions that will necessitate mastery, or complete understanding, of the situation in order to guarantee success. Because of the earlier analysis, this mastery can subsequently form the basis of a strategy.

Not only the strategy but also the strategic leader will have been born.

At times this process, which relies both on instinct and analysis, can cause the leader to take what may appear to be tough decisions. To some, they may appear to be unreasonable but, if clearly thought out, it should not be too difficult to persuade other people of the sense behind them. For example, Ingvar Kamparad, the founder of Ikea, who has also been described as 'Not only Ikea's chief strategy officer ... [he] also embodies the company's values and vision' (*Business Week*, 1997c), decided not to pass the organization on to his three sons as he was worried that they might quarrel over control of the company, thereby endangering it. Consequently, he transferred his equity into a charitable foundation in order to block any attempt by his sons to inherit it. Tough – but strategy has always been focus and hard choices! Other people who were less closely involved were quick to applaud this action.

## Creating and communicating the vision

This essential feature of both leadership and strategy has been dealt with in detail in Chapter 4. There is little more to be said about the subject other than the vision is where leadership and strategy merge. Strategies that are driven solely by visionless planners are almost bound to fail as they will be organized but directionless. By the same token, a leader without a strategy will either only be effective at the trans-actional level, or, to quote Shakespeare, be 'Full of sound and fury – signifying nothing!' (*Macbeth*).

But then, even the most meaningful and significant visions must be communi-cated. It is here, in the way that the leader chooses to develop and communicate the vision, that the seeds of success or failure are sown. It is all too easy to assume that other people share your enthusiasm, your passion – they may find it easier to share these strong emotions if they have had a say in the initial development of that vision. In all events, both passion and subtlety are required of the strategic leader and some of the necessary angles, 'angles of subtlety', are described below.

## Influencing organizational culture

In Chapter 5, we examined three levels of organizational culture: transactional, self-expression and mutuality. In a number of ways, these three levels correspond with the different stages of the development of leadership thinking; both involve a steady process of maturation. For a spirit of innovation, one that can transform an organization, to take root in the culture of an organization, I would contend that a mixture of self-expression and mutuality is required. In all events, a level of auton-omy and empowerment is necessary; without it creativity and innovation are unlikely to flourish other than as an expression of underground rebellion. So how should you, as a strategic leader, go about the difficult business of influencing the culture of your organization or department?

The answers to these questions lie both in acknowledging that it is now 'OK to think and act differently' and also in acting to build an accompanying resilience in the organization.

## A stimulated rather than a measured culture

We need to get one thing straight. This does not mean licence and it does not mean institutionalized rebellion. However, it does mean working towards a redefinition of the concept of 'operational effectiveness' – something that has often been regarded as an end in itself rather than as a means to an end.

A refreshing revolt against the straitjacket of operational effectiveness emerged in the 1997 IPD National Conference (IPD, 1997). Effectiveness as such was not challenged, rather the idea that this was all that mattered, that it was a defining metric for measuring the organization. 'Much more important is strategic positioning – the development of distinctive products or services, based on a unique combination of activities that allow a company to dominate a market or niche,' stated Michael Porter. He included concepts such as total quality management, benchmarking, business process re-engineering and even the learning organization within his definition. In pursuing them, he considered companies or the people within them to be becoming more and more like hamsters caught in their hamster wheels, running faster and faster for diminishing returns.

Professor Tony Hope (IPD, 1997) took up the theme and stated that budgets were often used as control tools producing 'irrelevant figures correct to two decimal figures'. He concluded that companies needed to decide what the right things to measure were in order to achieve competitive advantage and added that, 'You should stimulate your organization rather than control it'.

And how to achieve this stimulation? Well, for a start, a co-operative and motivated workforce is more likely both to work within sensible checks and measures as well as provide the spark that will help transform the organization. At the same conference, IPD Director-General Geoff Armstrong concluded the arguments against the hamster wheel when he stated, 'Companies rightly expect people at work to co-operate in the process of change and in achieving productivity and quality gains. But this co-operation won't be forthcoming if they are treated as an expendable source without respect' (IPD, 1997).

So, treat your people well, respect them and give them credit for having the intelligence to assist in formulating elements of the strategy as well as how it will be implemented. This message is by no means new but still bears repetition. If you listen to your people's views, ask them to listen to your views, share knowledge and the benefit of your research with them, then it is very likely that they will help you to mould the sort of company that you, they and your customers want to see. People who feel driven, who have decisions foisted upon them without consultation, are hardly likely to feel enthusiastic about the imposed direction. On the other hand, if they are consulted, if their views are taken into account, then their collective enthusiasm is likely to drive you towards the type of organization you want to see happen, faster than you would ever have realized.

Warren Bennis (1989) once stated that 'Leaders forge the future.' This undoubtably is the case but it is hard for the blacksmith to succeed without the co-operation of the horse and without a blacksmith's mate who understands what is going on!

## A resilient organization with resilient people

Mary Lynn Pulley (1997), writing for the Center for Creative Leadership, looked at the characteristics of resilient people, those who were able to cope well with job loss or continuing uncertainty. She found that these people had an ability to take control of their own career direction, had a strong sense of meaning (they were able to link their own strong sense of purpose to their daily work), had a strong sense of personal identity in so far that they recognized that there was a difference between who they were and what they did, had a strong personal and professional network and could also imagine how to apply their skills in a variety of settings. All the above talents were underpinned by a strong value system and a desire to learn what governed the standards they worked to. Pulley concluded that these people were survivors; they were able to thrive, whether or not they kept their jobs.

It should follow therefore that an organization staffed with resilient people will be less risk averse, more able to cope with both the pluses and minuses of change. It should also be better able to work to stretching targets as long as the values, purpose and overall strategy are made quite clear. It would therefore make sense to conclude that you can influence an organization's culture only if you carry its most important asset – the people – with you. If they are truly its most important asset then they will have values and opinions that in themselves will be of value. Link what they feel is important to your idea of where the organization should go and, no doubt after vigorous debate, you will achieve a consensus that will delineate the culture. Paradoxically, within that culture people will undoubtably define their own hamster wheels and probably pedal harder than ever – simply because these wheels are of their own making!

Perhaps this is the ideal culture to aim for!

## Motivating, inspiring and building trust

Much has been written in the past on motivation and it is certainly not the intention here to plough through the literature on the subject. Suffice it to say that most of it is valid and even though not all the theories say exactly the same thing, they are close enough to add to the sum total of common wisdom rather than contradict one another. Quite often in academic circles you will find a depressing tendency to put down one line of thought in favour of another and, especially, attempts to discredit the ideas that have been around the longest. This is rubbish – do the same people try to discredit great music, literature or religion, simply because it has been around for some time?

Consequently, I would like to base the focus here concerning the motivational aspects of transformational leadership on a quote from the beginning of the twentieth century. John Buchan, the author, stated, 'The job of a leader is not to create greatness in humanity but to elicit it, as the greatness is there already'.

For years, many organizations have been using the approach known as management by objectives. It is useful in that it provides a structure for action, planning and assessment. Objectives can be geared to the overarching strategy and whether goals are achieved or not can be used as a yardstick to ascertain whether both individuals and the organization are reaching their targets. The argument is that one should follow the other; if individuals reach their targets then, it follows, so should the organization. However, this approach does not go far enough; *people* are not simply motivated by reaching targets – what does motivate them are the *implications* of having reached those targets.

The implications themselves may be very varied. Will they be better off? Will their customers appreciate the value of their work? Will they have improved society, the state of mankind? Over and above all this, do they believe they are capable of achieving stretching targets, that the targets are worthwhile and that their leaders believe they are capable of excellence in all they do? There are numerous examples of people having achieved great things simply by believing in themselves. And where does self-belief come from? Usually from the knowledge that other people believe in you!

It is here that the main challenge to the leader lies. How can you foster the essential self-belief in others that will enable them to carry the strategy forward? The answer must lie in actively demonstrating your trust in other people, of overcommunicating that trust in order to ensure that the message is received loud and clear, and then at the same time agreeing stretching targets with them – because you know they can achieve them! After that, it is a question of delegating, agreeing responsibility levels and continually demonstrating your faith in their ability. This in no way obviates the need to coach or mentor; in fact it may well make these activities more necessary.

George Bernard Shaw in his famous play *Pygmalion* gave Eliza Doolittle the words to best describe the positive or negative effects on the follower of different levels of expectation from above. She explained, 'The difference between a lady and a flower girl is not how she behaves, but how she is treated. If treated as a flower girl she will always be one; if treated as a lady, then she will become one'. Of course, the great flaw in the arrogant Professor Higgins was that he only focused on the outcome of his wager and did not realize until it was almost too late that he was simply polishing a stone that had been precious all along.

To bring the concept back into a business scenario, the strategy requires a vision; the vision should be stretching and require high expectations of all concerned. It could be argued that the fulfilment of the expectations incorporated within the strategy is the sole reason for the organization's existence. Consequently, an atmosphere of positive expectations backed up by the right sort of leadership approach is probably one of the most powerful and sustainable sources of competitive advantage – therefore, developing and building positive expectations both of and among staff may be one of the most important things a strategic leader can do.

But then the question arises – how do you do it? There are a number of approaches, in fact it would be easy to fill a whole book with them; so here are just a few:

1.  Coach, mentor, and seek every opportunity to do so.

2.  Make sure that your mouth and feet are pointing in the same direction. For example, there is no point in telling your people that they are the most talented in the industry and then bringing people in from outside at higher levels. If you are forced to do this, you had better line up some compelling arguments.

3.  'Catch people doing something right' said Kenneth Blanchard (Blanchard and Johnson, 1983). And when you do so, praise them. Praise is the cheapest management tool, one of the most effective and one of the least used.

4.  Foster a culture that embraces learning while at the same time encouraging diversity of approach and opinion. It is when this happens that true creativity and the realization of people's positive expectations can be harnessed to implement strategies effectively and with commitment.

5.  When working with teams, do not try to dominate them but take on the role of creative group catalyst. This is a facilitative approach where the leader may ask stimulating questions (see Chapters 2 and 3 for the type of questions you could ask), give the team feedback and help them when they are 'blocked'. A vital component of facilitation is that the leader does not try to railroad the discussion to a previously defined end. This approach, however, does not involve abdication of authority (in the end you probably have the right to disregard what the team members are saying), instead it enhances your authority by increasing the overall talent and motivation of your team. Lao Tse, the Chinese philosopher, put it succinctly, 'Sometimes you must give your power away in order to enhance it.'

## Balancing your own approach

Of course, it is easy to give advice but when the pressure is on to make a strategy 'happen', when others are after you for results, when you are convinced that your vision is inspired and that the strategy is not only right but essential, when you are consumed by the passion of leadership, then it is easy to become frustrated with the pace at which others learn, or needled when they do not always agree with you. Herein lies one of the great dilemmas of leadership. Leaders are expected to show energy, commitment, passion and it is that very passion that can liberate the minds and hearts of others. However, these same talents can become stumbling blocks if taken to excess, if not balanced by an alternative perspective.

One of the key talents of an effective strategic leader, one who needs to be able to play the long game, is to be able to balance the forces within by an equally powerful counter-force in such a way as to prevent the initial force becoming excessive. The combination of balanced forces can then become a powerful source of additional strength to you as a leader. Some of the key driving forces/talents that contribute to making a strategic leader are far-sightedness, passion, perseverance, hardiness, need to command and control, clear process focus and a determined output focus. I have identified a counteracting force for each of the above and set them out in the yin/yang of strategic leadership – a concept that first struck me when working in the Far East.

## The yin/yang of strategic leadership

### Far sight and insight
It is necessary for the strategic leader to be able to look ahead, to analyse, to scan the business and economic horizons for trends, impending changes and opportunities. However, if the ability to look ahead is not coupled with an insight into why things are happening as opposed simply to a preview as to what might happen, then analysis will be incomplete. It may be accurate in the immediate future but is unlikely to foretell events much beyond. So, there is a need to ask lots of questions that demand to know 'What would be the consequences of' or 'What might happen next' as well as 'What are the underlying causes of the observable trends?' Questions such as these will add a whole new dimension to your strategic thinking.

### Passion and compassion
It is all too easy for the passion that gives life to the vision and a driving energy to the strategy to become intolerance – for the overwhelming conviction of what is necessary to make the leader forget that there are people involved in the equation. The process of balancing the passion with compassion means that you must acknowledge other people's attitudes, expectations and fears. This does not obviate you from the responsibility of making tough decisions but does mean that you should never forget that these decisions directly affect other people's lives (and sometimes the lives of whole communities) – act with this in mind.

### Perseverance and perspective
Tenacity, the ability to see things through to the end, is an admirable quality. However, if it means a dogged, short-sighted attitude of 'I've started so I'll finish – no matter what!' then it can become a definite weakness and it must be countered with an ample measure of perspective. The perspective is achieved by deliberately standing back and asking yourself a new set of difficult questions, 'Is the problem the same one that I set out to tackle or have things changed? Is a new strategy called for? What else could we be doing to get results?' The resultant new perspective should mean that you achieve a new focus on the situation; one that tempers the quality of perseverance making it much more likely to produce results.

### Hardiness and humility
In order to drive a strategy you must be able not only to make the tough decision, to exercise the hard choice, but also to be tough enough to accept criticism, face up to failure and admit blame where blame is due. The person who is capable of pushing

ahead despite the odds is a valuable asset anywhere but there is always a danger that this sort of person can become arrogant, drunk with success and regard other people as mere pawns in the game. True leaders are respected for their humanity and this involves avoiding the seductive trap of starting to believe that you are better than other people and consequently displaying patience and empathy as well as being open to discussion and feedback. The concept of the 'leader servant' is by no means a new concept but it is a powerful one.

### Command and control and trust and conviction

As mentioned earlier in this chapter, the art of adopting the right style of leadership to match the situation is vital. However, all too often we see management adopting a 'tell' style no matter what the circumstances. Without doubt this style has its place but is not a style that is likely to develop either the skills or commitment of followers. Command and control should be a weapon that is always there and available but seldom unsheathed. Instead, the maxim 'Giving trust breeds trust' should hold centre stage. If people know why they are being asked to do something and are also given latitude in the way that they do it, then they will be both flattered as well as more committed to the task in hand.

### Process focus and results focus

What follows may sound heretical, especially to management trainers who love to coach people on the importance of getting the process right. The concept that it is *how you do it* that is all-important is a good one. Indeed, a good process in addressing a task is far more likely to obtain the desired results than a poor one. However, process is not all and in the end it is the final result that counts. A colleague of mine and I often have good-natured disputes when judging the results of business games on management training courses. He wants to award the prize to the team that has demonstrated the best process during the event, while I, who have not always been as close to the process, want to make the award to the team that have produced the best final result. Best process and best end result do not always go hand in hand, so listen to your heretics, see whether the rules can be bent and strike the right balance.

### Output focus and value focus

A good definition of a cynic is someone who knows the cost of everything and the value of nothing. By the same token (and almost in contradiction to the previous paragraph) do not be seduced by the siren voices that urge you to go just for output, volume, quick profit and big dividends for investors. In the long term, it is the *value* that an organization can add that makes a difference and gives it staying power. This value can be measured both by the metric of return on assets managed but also by the true value that the product or service can add to the organization's clients, or hopefully even to the larger community as a whole. Another key strategic question should therefore be about asking where the long-term value may be found and how it can be both demonstrated and maintained.

## Persuading other people

Persuasion, the art of getting others to see your point of view, if really done well can succeed in converting them not only to being enthusiastic about what you have in mind, but also to join you in the crusade. Much excellent work has been done on describing styles and approaches to persuasion (see Eales-White, 1992). Here we will concentrate not so much on the interpersonal styles as on an overall strategy for successful persuasion. Suffice it to say, the ability to be persuasive is an essential tool in the strategic leader's toolkit.

### A strategy for persuasion

The first half of the strategy involves analysis and preparation. The importance of this groundwork cannot be over-emphasized.

1.  Work out your objectives. You must be clear as to what you want to achieve – how else can you communicate it powerfully to someone else?

2.  Think empathetically. What does the other person want? What might be worrying that person? Is there anything that you can offer which will match these wants or concerns and increase the effectiveness of your approach?

3.  Prepare your presentation. This is not just your line of argument but also how you will deliver it. You must analyse what is most likely to work with the particular person, or persons, you have in mind. What will work in this case? Appeals to logic? Appeal to group consensus? Or is a harder style required? Try to recall the kind of language and logic that the other person uses; if he or she tends to use a particular approach then it is quite likely that a similar approach will work on them.

The second stage of the strategy is the meeting itself.

4.  Find out where the other person is coming from. Ask questions, find out their views and adjust your approach according to what you see and hear.

5.  Share your views. Tell that person why you hold such views and elicit the reasons for any objections that they may have.

6.  Sell the benefits. You will have good reasons for your plans. Think in terms of the benefits that there may be for the other person rather than just of the bald facts of your case. Think WIFMs, we all have them. It stands for 'What's in it for me?' What might be the other person's WIFMs?

7.  Make the other person curious. If you can succeed here, you are halfway there; they will start to become involved despite themselves and involvement is a major step towards commitment.

8.  Leave them a way out. Be tactful; if you so comprehensively defeat all the other person's counter-arguments that they feel mentally pillaged, they may

stubbornly stick to their position simply to preserve their self-esteem. So let them have their say and concede to valid points – this tactic will probably strengthen your long-term position.

9.  Get agreement and then move on. Once you have got agreement, agree what has been agreed, document it if appropriate and confirm what actions need to be taken. Then break off the conversation and move on. If you hang around for a 'general chat' then you may suddenly find yourself back in the original argument again.

10. Evaluate. If you have been successful, think hard about what worked. Learn from it, build on it and repeat that approach in the future.

## Driving forward appropriate strategies

In the end, the strategy must succeed. Too many failed strategies will inevitably mean the end of the organization and with it the demise of the strategic leader.

In order to grow the business, to reach the stretching goals implied by the vision, it is necessary to choose the right strategy based on sound evaluation of both the long-term and the more immediate future. This necessitates the right sort of analysis of product or marketplace and thereafter development of the strategy by the use of a model of strategic health and direction, such as has been put forward in this book. But the overall strategy has to be driven, or to put it more exactly, led. The following guidelines for strategic leadership give the essential steps in this process. All the steps are necessary and complementary; in describing them I have also detailed the probable consequences of ignoring that particular step.

- *Challenge the status quo*   Seek a new direction. If this is not done, others will not feel any need for change and any subsequent strategy is likely to be still-born.

- *Develop a vision for the future*   Without a vision there can be no common sense of direction, no communicated passion from the leader and no energy in reply from the followers. No channels of energy, no strategy.

- *Lead the way*   When devising the overall shape of the strategy, as well as showing interest and involvement in its implementation, it is vital to be visible. All too often high D-brain visionaries have moved on to dream about the next grand scheme, long before the current strategy has begun to show results. Without ongoing and committed visibility a credibility gap will open up and the work on the strategy will run out of steam.

- *Work a strategy model*   Let others know what stage has been reached in that model. If this is not done there is likely to be confusion and poor co-ordination.

- *Be focused on quality*   At a more detailed level make sure you understand what is going on. Tread the narrow path between interest and interference with care, remembering the devil is in the detail. Lack of process focus will endanger quality of output.

- *Empower others*   Omit this step and the strategy will flounder due to people's inability to understand and to use strategic tools and solve problems, or due to their lack of competence or commitment to enact the strategy.

- *Encourage and inspire*   Feedback on progress, praise and restatement of the vision are all vital. Without them, the individual processes, accountabilities and objectives that contribute to the overall strategy start to go off the rails, resulting in frustration all round.

'For the want of a nail, the shoe was lost, for the want of a shoe the horse was lost, for the want of a horse the kingdom was lost...' Many of these elements may appear insignificant in comparison to the sweeping panorama of a grand strategy. They are, nevertheless, the key components of that vital element of both politics and business – strategic leadership.

## Conclusion

In this chapter we have dealt with the crucial interaction between the leader, the strategy and members of the organization – the followers – the people who have the vital job of making the strategy happen. The plan for driving home the strategy illustrated above has summarized many of the key points within this chapter and has tended to focus on the people element of the strategy. This theme has cropped up in several other chapters. The fact is that strategies are about people, either as leaders, managers, technicians, followers, customers or members of the world community. Whatever the angle, get the people side right and the different elements of the strategy will start to fall into place. In Chapter 8, we will concentrate on the final actions that need to be completed in order to pull the whole strategy together – the final push to success!

## Action points for consideration

- Ask yourself what stage in the process of development of leadership you have reached. What new competencies might you need to develop in order to move ahead?

- Your mind may be open, but ask yourself as a leader what steps you have taken to open other people's minds.

- Think about the leadership within your own organization. To what extent are people consulted or involved in both the visioning process as well as that of implementing change? If they are acting more like hamsters, ask yourself what can be done about it.

- Take every opportunity to be a coach, facilitator and mentor. Recognize other people's talents and their potential to both conceiving and implementing strategies.

- Examine yourself and your approaches to situations. Have you got the yin/yang balance right?

- Look for opportunities to persuade other people rather than relying on giving orders. At the same time analyse your own potential effectiveness as a persuader.

- Remember that leaders usually start by challenging the *status quo*. Ask yourself what you are taking for granted.

# Chapter 8

# The final push to success

As a vast body of thinking individuals, mankind has, at the very centre of its being, the capability to be strategic. That does not mean to say that we are all strategic the whole of the time but, just as so many of us have it in us to be leaders and to develop ourselves as leaders, so it follows that we have the ability to be strategic. It is there, it is one of the things that differentiates us from the animal world.

In addition, the processes of strategic analysis and action have been available to the human race for centuries and the results of both past and present strategies are all around us, affecting us every day of our lives. The political boundaries that delineate the nations in which we live, the freedoms we enjoy, the products we consume are all the results of past strategies, while many issues such as the debate over a single European currency, the economic relationship of the West with the economies of the Pacific rim, the dilemma about what to do about Iraq's arsenal – these are all part and parcel of current strategies that have yet to run their full course.

Yet not all strategies succeed by any means. It is estimated that about 70 per cent of all strategic initiatives fail; a sober statistic indeed and it is not difficult to point out telling and recent examples. In the City of London, the computer system Taurus was going to change the face of financial settlements; it was never implemented although the cost to banks in setting up for it was enormous. Also in Britain, the advanced passenger train met all technical requirements for speed and looked certain to be a winner until early journeys showed that it was not able to negotiate bends successfully. Nor are failed strategies a purely British phenomenon – even the great Mercedes Benz was embarrassed when its new small car proved so unstable that it had to be withdrawn from sale to the public, at a stroke damaging severely the organization's strategy to make big inroads into the small car market.

So, we are surrounded by the results of strategies. While we may smile at some of the more amusing failures, it is the successful strategies that have a lasting influence. So what is it that gives a strategy the extra power to succeed? At the same time, what are the components of failure and how can they be avoided? In this chapter, we will look at why some strategies fail and then go on to look at some of the main components of risk management as a means of anticipating and avoiding complications.

At a personal level, we will examine how the individual strategist can become trapped by dilemmas on the interpersonal side of strategy implementation and will put forward a means of breaking the stranglehold of these dilemmas. This can be done by looking at how conflict between individuals can get in the way – as can organizational politics and the games that people play. These all can frustrate the best laid plans. In each case tactics for overcoming these problems will be put forward, as the overall ambition for any strategist must be that of successful implementation. But first of all; why do so many strategies fail?

# Reasons for failure – many, varied and avoidable

Of course, some strategies may be doomed to fail from the moment they are conceived. Unanticipated events or the superior strategies and products of competitors can stop even the most thoroughly thought through strategies in their tracks. But this need not always be the case and an overall success rate of only 30 per cent for all strategies launched is, to put it mildly, lamentable. Of course, the statistic itself may be suspect; after all, what is success? And should partial success be labelled success or failure? A recent spoof on statistical analysis recently declared with great tongue-in-cheek authority that 82.3 per cent of all statistical statements were suspect! I tend to agree!!

On the other hand, there do appear to be some common causes of failure, many of them avoidable and most related to human error at some part of the overall strategy process.

### Poor analysis

A crucial stage, as if you get this wrong then the whole strategy can get off to a false start. There is the old story about the American who is lost in the middle of Ireland and stops an old gentleman to ask the way to Dublin. The man stops to think, puffs on his pipe and then announces with great authority, 'Well, surr, if I was trying to get to Dublin, I certainly wouldn't be starting from here.' If we can untangle the logic of that reply, it is the same with many strategies. What it is they incorporate, what sub-plans they hold, may well depend on where you estimate yourselves to be at the start. So, it is necessary to devote time and energy to the initial stage – it may not be as exciting as conceiving the big picture or as exciting as action; but nevertheless it is vital.

### Incoherent formulation

If the end goal and the plans to achieve it are not well thought through the whole initiative will be doomed to failure. Afterwards people might say that it was not a good idea in the first place or that it only appeared to be a quick fix. If the vision and the key tasks and processes are not defined in detail then the strategy is not going to work, even with the most willing and effective management team. For example, a salesforce will waste its energy if there has been insufficient analysis of the market and inaccurate targeting of retailers or customers. Big pictures on their own do not deliver the goods!

## Lax evaluation

If this phase of the strategy does not take place before anything is done and if it does not continue to happen throughout the entire roll-out phase, then unanticipated problems are likely to arise and will dog the implementation project throughout its life. Initially the problems will stem from poor analysis of the external situation which is often due to insufficient time being devoted to asking questions and 'what iffing'. Consequently those responsible for deciding the key phases of the strategy, for selecting the vital actions that constitute it, will have a poor understanding of both the business context and the potential pitfalls in which it must be launched, as well as being even less prepared for any changes in that context.

## Haphazard implementation

Many of the problems inherent in the implementation of a strategy do not stem from the intrinsic value of the strategy itself but from the way in which it is implemented. For a start, if the essential purpose of the strategy has not been communicated then it is hard to see how people can work out how they can contribute to it. More often, however, the vision, purpose and goals of the strategy are made known but the roles and responsibilities of those who should be involved in making it happen are not clarified. The clear communication of specific responsibilities for the successful implementation of the organization's strategy may seem such an obvious requirement that it is hard to see how this essential step can be forgotten. But forgotten it often is. Or even worse, responsibilities are often partially clarified, leading to confusion, conflict and eventual inertia among key employees. Lack of clarity usually leads to risk aversion.

As a test, it is worth asking yourself whether you are quite clear what the overall strategy of your organization is, what your specific responsibilities are in connection with them and how those responsibilities connect to and add to those of your colleagues.

Subject yourself to the elevator test; you meet someone whom you have not met for several years, just as you are both boarding an elevator. Your old friend asks you who you are now working for and to describe the organization's main purpose as well as your role in helping it to achieve its goals. If you are unable to come up with immediate and specific answers to those questions (by the time you get to floor 10), then maybe your own organization is failing here.

Finally, there is what might be called the frantic seagull syndrome. Top management fly in, make a lot of noise in communicating the BHAG, set a number of strategic objectives and then disappear with the wind – to be heard no more. They have made and communicated decisions but do not appear to be involved with or interested in their implementation. Consequently, those left holding the baby feel not so much empowered as sprinkled with guano! The hapless implementers sit and await the arrival of the next fad with trepidation, wondering whether they will be capable of clearing up future messes.

### Unheeded control

Strategies can run out of steam, go over budget and fail in a number of ways if not controlled. Here, financial information, project updates and both the collection and dissemination of facts and figures are vital. The key fact here is that the data must be seen as useful both to those responsible for collecting it and to those providing it. When the information is regarded as useful by all rather than just some bureau-cratic exercise, then and only then will it prove to be an apt factor in motivating people, curbing excesses and making strategies successful. A useful analogy is that of the controls of an aircraft – they are all necessary and provide the pilot with essential information about the aircraft's well-being and progress; and without which future manoeuvres are not attempted. When control information is seen as this vital and is used in this way both projects and strategies are likely to be far more successful.

And of course, control information is vital in the planning and control of risk but is just a part of the overall discipline of risk management.

# Risk management

While not always found as an element of strategic planning, just how well risks are calculated and managed can make a huge difference to the overall success of a strategy as well as the projects that comprise it. Indeed, the Cadbury report (1992) on corporate governance recommended that boards should have risk management policies in place, built on good internal controls. In the aftermath of disasters such as the Barings fiasco, this is good advice indeed: but what exactly is meant by risk and risk management?

Risk has been defined as 'exposure to adversity or chance of loss; possibility of loss or outcome different than expected'. It could also be regarded as the quantifi-able probability that something will or will not happen and here those trying to assess the risk look for precedents or similar situations in order to estimate these probabilities. In the light of these definitions, risk management could be defined as the science of dealing with the pure risk faced by individuals and businesses (as in life insurance), and as the art of recognizing the existence of direct or indirect threats, thereby determining their likely impact on the organization and thereafter taking action to control those threats – here both intuitive foresight as well as scientific forecasting can be brought into play. However, above all else, risk management should be an attitude of mind that permeates all major decisions and processes. It is about asking 'What if?' questions in a variety of different contexts in order to improve the scope of thinking about the future, to gain knowledge and to have a better idea of the range of possible outcomes in any given situation.

Risk management as a discipline of mind is becoming more necessary as both societies and the business environment become less stable and harder to predict as economies and institutions become more interdependent globally. The collapse of a stockbroking firm in Tokyo may well have profound effects in Europe and the US – something that would have been unthinkable a few short years ago. So, in times when changes come faster and are less predictable, it is necessary for managers to be able to take quick corrective measures – at the same time it is harder and takes more time to change a major strategic direction and so the level of risk inherent in any strategy must be measured. It is necessary to look at projects in terms of the risks they involve, not simply at what they cost, as unforeseen risks will represent unsubstantial but potentially significant costs. And success lies with those who dare – in future the willingness to take risks will be a key differentiator of both companies and individuals; risk management will increasingly be seen as a key part of a manager's role as well as a key element of business strategy. However, the crucial question still remains; how do you analyse, control and 'manage' the risks involved?

In looking at risk management there is one overarching truth. It is not possible to eliminate risks completely, but you can manage and control them. Consequently, the objectives of risk management are to ensure that risks are:

- Identified as early as possible.
- Realistically assessed.
- Actively managed by taking appropriate actions.

The subsequent process of risk management, for which I am indebted to my colleague John Coppendale of the PA Consulting Group, then goes as follows:

At the start of a course of action:

1. *Put together a risk identification team and brainstorm potential risks*   Here it is best to select people for their different skills and also their different aptitudes. For example, a team comprised principally of members with strong D-brain preferences would probably be too preoccupied with long-term possibilities rather than the risks involved in getting there. They would need some cautious B-brain input or some questioning A-brain logic.

2. *Classify the risk into broad subject areas*   These, for example, might be technical, financial, market movement, dependence on third parties, resource availability, possibility of timescale slippage.

3. *Define the probability and impact*   This can be done by debating the probability of each risk occurring and the impact on events if it does occur. Both probability and impact can be rated on a scale of low, medium or high in each case and by plotting them onto a graph which enables each risk to be more fully

located and assessed. As can be seen in Figure 8.1, the overall risk vulnerability is then starkly portrayed and the level of risk awareness is heightened. A course of action may have a large number of small inherent risks with low probability of occurrence, or on the other hand, just one or two major risks with a very high probability. In each case, the way forward will probably be very different.

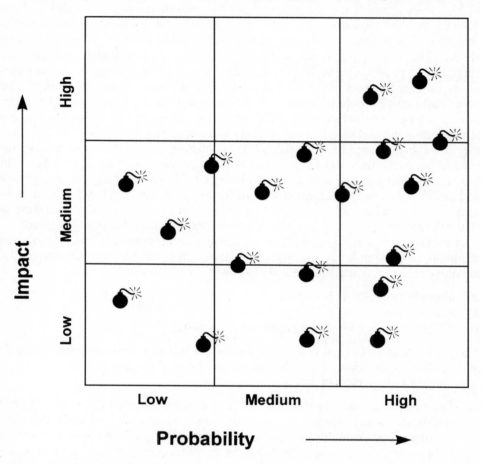

**Figure 8.1     The risk matrix: creating risk awareness**

4.  *Develop an action plan for each identified risk*   The plan should set out to reduce the chances of whatever actually constitutes the risk taking place and to put contingency measures into place should the threat actually happen. Both sets of actions are necessary and interdependent. For example, it is wise to take all precautions against fire in a hotel but foolish to take out the fire escapes because initial precautions have been taken. Each action plan should specify individual responsibilities and reporting dates for progress updates.

5.  *Review the progress*   Examine the risk management accountabilities against the plan incorporated in step 4 and use the reviews to update the assessment of risks on a regular basis.

The process itself is quite simple but the rigour implied in the steps incorporated within it may be quite demanding. Demanding? Maybe, but ever necessary. Rigorous? Most certainly, and always essential.

To summarize, in looking at the reasons why projects fail, it is usually because one step in the overall strategic process has been omitted or because a particular form of thinking has been either underused or overused. On the other hand risks may not have been anticipated with the result that timely steps were not taken to manage them.

If effort is put in to anticipate and manage risks at the start of the implementation process then it is very likely that the subsequent roll-out will be much smoother. However, this effort may well be regarded as 'needless hassle' by those who prefer to charge into action. On the other hand, there are those who prefer to anticipate and deal with risks as each different stage of the strategy roll-out draws near. For them, the hassle will not peak but may well be spread out fairly evenly throughout the process. Then there are those who prefer not to think about risk and for them the hassle will probably peak several times during the implementation phase with an inevitable hiatus close to the final stages. The three different outcomes are illustrated in Figure 8.2, illustrating the necessity of building in an element of risk management as a crucial part of any strategy implementation process or plan.

While good processes are vital, in the end, however, the success or failure of a strategy often depends upon the people involved, their characters and the way in which they interact with one another. Now complications such as interpersonal conflict or organizational politics raise their ugly heads. Many good strategies have floundered upon these rocks, and as investors, in the end, usually put their money on people rather than strategies *per se*, it is necessary to look at these basic human issues in the final assessment of the essential factors necessary to guarantee healthy progress in the final push to success.

## Conflict and politics

When a strategy is conceived, it is conceived with a view to changing something. It involves the application of focus and the making of hard choices and as part of both this focus and exercise of the hard choices, it will arouse ambitions and expectations as well as counter-reactions and fears. In other words, the implementation of a strategy is likely to create the conditions for both open conflict between the individuals involved, as well as the more hidden machinations of political manoeuvring. Many a well-conceived strategy has been derailed by the fact that the person responsible for its implementation has not been able to cope with interpersonal conflict or has been frustrated by political game-playing. So it is therefore necessary to look at the implications of these traps as well as how to deal with them as crucial elements in the implementation process.

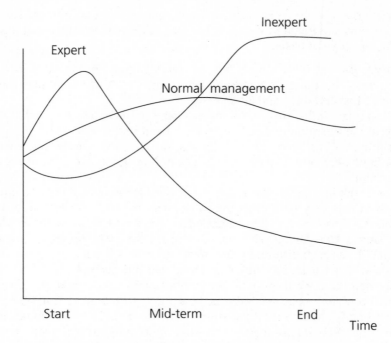

- Experts invest effort and hassle at the start and it steadily decreases.
- Normal strategic managers are faced with a steady level of hassle.
- Inexperts do not anticipate risks and after a false dawn are faced with constantly increasing levels of hassle.

**Figure 8.2     Consequences of different approaches to risk management**

## Conflict

People will oppose each other over the division of resources, on differences of opinion about how things should be done and on a whole host of other issues – not least of which might well be whether the strategy should be started in the first place. It is a mistake, however, to believe that all conflict is undesirable; it can be invaluable in helping to sort out the *what* of focus as well as the *what, where, how* and *why* of the hard choices. While it can be uncomfortable, it can have a positive function especially when it is healthy and those involved are prepared to debate the issue. It is when the conflict is unhealthy that more effort is needed to resolve it positively.

Conflict can be considered to be healthy when those involved want to reach a solution to the issue in question, are prepared to argue (perhaps vigorously) but in the end want to reach a solution and are prepared to consider a compromise. During the debate, both sides will listen to each other, will share ideas and perhaps find that the initial conflict has evolved into a negotiation where there is every chance of a settlement that will satisfy everyone. The conflict is unhealthy where neither side is prepared to compromise or to listen to the other's views. Here, scant respect will be paid to the other side and the debate may well descend into point-scoring and aggression.

When you find yourself in conflict with someone else, it is all too easy to become embroiled in emotion. While this is understandable, it will not help you resolve the issue. So, the first step is to detach yourself from the emotion of it all, to stand back, to look at the problem rather than the person involved and to seek clarity. If it is not possible to physically get away from the conflict, try to relax and try not to show any overt aggression towards the other person; this will only lead to escalation and to an attack/defence spiral of argument. Very often it is useful to change the environment, to suggest that the conversation continues on neutral territory and when it does continue, to listen hard and go for clarity by asking as many questions as possible. Once again open questions can help you to better analyse the whole situation and to get a fuller understanding of the other person's views.

It is surprising how conflict can be defused if one of the parties remains calm and reasonable; in fact, just taking this stance may well give you an advantage. Once you have heard the other person out it is time to share your views. State your views of the person or their behaviour (not their character!) and ensure that you have been understood. It is now time to look for a way forward and you could start by asking the other person what they think should happen. Without sacrificing your ideals or core values, look for the win–win position where both people feel that they have achieved the best out of the situation given all the factors involved. In win–win situations both sides focus on reaching a satisfactory outcome as well as maintaining the relationship between each other. Once agreement has been reached it is important to 'agree what you have just agreed' – this will prevent you both finding yourselves in conflict again over the same issue because of some trivial misunderstanding.

Of course, you will from time to time come up against the totally unreasonable individual, the person who will not listen to reason under any circumstances. We have all met this sort of person before and the best tactic is total avoidance (and it is amazing how often they are lonely, isolated characters). Where this is not possible, you will need to be assertive and if necessary to look for allies as people of this sort can delay or destroy good strategies almost indefinitely. 'There are none so blind as those who will not see' is an old adage illustrated in Northern Ireland, Bosnia and other places where unreasonable people ensure that progress towards reason and harmony is impossible.

But then there is a third sort of conflict. A less obvious form that nevertheless can frustrate strategies, hamper individuals and even bring down careers. It is the form of conflict that, by its very nature, can present you with the most complicated array of dilemmas – the conflict that masquerades in the form of organizational politics.

## Politics – The art of survival

It was Benjamin Franklin who coined the saying 'In this world nothing can be said to be certain, except death and taxes'. But anybody who has ever worked in an organization will probably add a third element to the list – organizational politics. Avoiding any of the three is just downright impossible no matter how important you are; however, if you do not try to anticipate organizational politics, as Julius Caesar found out, by the time you get to say *'Et tu Brute?'* it is usually too late to do anything about it!

Now, while conflict between individuals is usually overt, in the open and often noisy, there is another form of conflict which is often silent, less obvious and less often discussed. Yet, like the poor, it is always with us despite the fact that little has been written about it and it is not often openly discussed. Could this be because people find the subject distasteful or because they think it is unworthy of attention? It is certainly not found in the syllabus of any MBA programme or management course that I have come across and the sensible reaction must be 'What an opportunity wasted!' It is probable that more strategies have floundered and more careers come to grief because of organizational politics than for any other reason.

On the other hand people have been aware of political game-playing since the beginning of time, or at least since the beginning of organized life. It was Socrates who first coined the phrase 'political animals' while much later Charles Darwin was to declare that 'All things start in vision and mystery and end in politics' – a stark reminder for leaders of all persuasions! So what should you do when you are confronted with or suspect organizational politics? Do you deny its existence? Avoid it? Rise above it? Accommodate it by indulging in it yourself? Whatever stance you take you will be presented with dilemmas – by not playing the game do you let yourself down, while by playing it, do you sacrifice your own integrity thereby letting yourself down in possibly more far-reaching ways?

These are difficult questions. Indeed, as a management trainer, a high proportion of the extra-curricular questions (that is, those asked in the bar at the end of the day) focus on these thorny issues. The short answer to the integrity question is a categorical 'No! Never, sacrifice it'. However, is it possible to retain your integrity and still be 'politically smart'? There are a number of pointers to the fact that this is both possible and desirable. For example, in the US the Center for Creative Leadership conducted a study of the reasons why fast-track managers derailed. They found that young executives often displayed characteristics of extreme ambition, drove themselves and other people hard, and did not often care what others thought of them. Very often these characteristics manifested themselves in political manoeuvres but paradoxically it was those very same characteristics that undermined them later in their careers. Senior managers needed to be more strategic, take longer-term perspectives and be more skilful and considerate in dealing with people. Those who remained over-ambitious, abrasive and willing to do anything tended to come unstuck. In short, those who lived by the sword, died by the sword.

Further light in the integrity versus survival dilemma is shed by an approach developed at Birmingham University and further defined at Cranfield University, which divided people up into four different animal groups when it came to politics. The criteria for the grouping depended on whether they were interested and informed about what was going on politically in their organization and the extent to which they put themselves or the company first. The sheep, the researchers discovered, did not know what was going on but were loyal, hardworking and put the organization first. They tended to be cannon fodder. Donkeys, on the other hand, also did not know what was going on but put themselves first, often grumbled and were stubborn about adapting to changes – they were usually given more work and overlooked when it came to promotion.

A far more positive animal was the wise owl who knew exactly what was going on, who was up to what and who was doing what to whom – but did not indulge. They were loyal to the organization and had high integrity. They did not always reach the top but they did enjoy high respect from colleagues and were more secure than most. Finally there were the foxes. Foxes knew and played all the political games and, being ambitious, always put their own interests before those of other people as well as the organization itself.

So what is the best position to be in? Which animal would you choose to be? Having asked that question of a large number of managers of different nationalities, the answer invariably is that you need to behave like an owl while knowing how to think like a fox. In other words, without sacrificing your own integrity or self-respect, you need to know the games and how they are played in order to counter the games that might be played against you.

But what are the games, what is it that the foxes do? The following represents some of the more common ploys that I have observed; I am sure that the list is by no means complete and you may care to add to it from your own experiences.

- Discrediting someone else, implying that what they did was 'courageous' – that is, foolish – or damning with faint praise.

- Hoarding information and either using it to one's own advantage or releasing it only when you have benefited from it in some way.

- Manipulating meetings – never giving straight answers and using meetings to promote one's own viewpoint.

- Spending inordinate amounts of energy to impress, please and flatter those more senior. Some quite rude adjectives are used to describe this sort of behaviour, often concerned with the colour of the individual's nose!

- Spreading rumours to undermine other people's initiatives. Even if false, the harm has been done.

- Playing power games between departments and by implication dragging all those who work for those departments into the game.

- Abusing one's power by putting colleagues and subordinates into difficult positions, often passing the onus of making one's own difficult decisions on to them.

- Covering up one's own mistakes and trying to shift the blame for them onto other people.

- Inordinate hogging of the limelight and somehow claiming promising initiatives as one's own!

- On the other hand, never around when things go badly wrong, yet always first to say, 'I told you so'.

So how do you counter these ploys, manoeuvrings and manipulations? Of course, there can be no one right answer but the following general strategies may be helpful as an overall guide:

- Be aware – understand the opportunities for politicking that the foxes might seize.

- Study the politicians; look for trends, common characteristics and repeat behaviours. From this learn to anticipate what they might get up to.

- Ask yourself why these people are playing politics; could it be due to ambition, boredom, fear, love of power or even love of mischief? Knowledge of motive may well lead to detection and prevention, as Sherlock Holmes would tell you.

- Try to defuse situations where possible. Is it possible to insist on straightforwardness on all sides without this appearing to be appeasement?

- If that does not work, approach possible allies and go for strength in unity.

- Finally, there is the option of confronting the issue with Mr or Ms Fox; show that you understand what is going on. But be sure that you are on firm ground before you start. As this may result in conflict of a more open kind, choose your subject carefully, assess the other person's strengths and weaknesses, and be sure your facts are correct.

But this in itself is beginning to sound political. The fact is that there are no easy answers, although there can be guidelines. In the end, in order to prosper, for your strategies to be effective, you must be 'aware' and learn to apply this awareness in ways that enforce your position rather than detract from it. All your skill in questioning, listening and, above all, in using your intuition must be fully deployed to ensure that you are effective no matter what the situation. Keeping your antennae out at all times, having a few countermeasures in your kit bag, need not compromise your integrity, does not mean that you necessarily become a fox – but it does make you a better owl.

But now we have in fact moved into the subject of personal development – something that is absolutely necessary if you wish to become more effective as a strategist.

# Developing yourself as a strategist

If the methodology of strategic analysis has been available to the human race for centuries, then by the same token the tools for developing yourself as a strategist have been available for the same length of time. Many have exercised them unconsciously while others have been more methodical in their approach. It is fortunate for the human race that some, like Hitler, while undoubtedly strategic by nature, were extremely flawed when it came to the finer points of implementation. So, the line between being strategic, convincing others and making the strategic plan happen is a thin one. In the end, final success is down to you, the individual.

All of the elements required to ensure successful conception, such as thinking differently, asking searching questions, seeking to change and improve the *status quo*, have already been described earlier in this book. The talents needed to ensure implementation, such as adopting the right leadership style, managing change, working the processes and strategic models, have been described alongside other necessities such as the need to manage risk and the interpersonal complexities within organizations. In fact, the process of learning to work the models, of becoming adept at the interpersonal elements, are all integral to your holistic development as a strategist as opposed to your development as a planner.

So what is missing?

In the end, your success depends upon how well you carry out the skills and competencies described above. So far the role that luck plays in defining the success or failure of a strategy has not been dealt with – on the other hand, it is a well-known fact that you tend to make your own luck through determination, practice and sheer hard work. But there is a final element, and that is judgement. This may be a part of wisdom, itself a key element of leadership, but in the end it is something more. Judgement could be described as the ability to make decisions and the ability to use one's skills, despite having imperfect information and sometimes without the advice or backing of those around you.

For example, judgement will play a vital role in defining how you set out to communicate the strategy to other people and attempt to motivate them. If the strategy involves changes that are not clearly communicated or articulated, then it will not be surprising if people within the organization are not frantically enthusiastic about carrying out the tasks involved in implementing the strategic initiative. This book started with a number of military definitions of strategy and, although it has principally concentrated on commercial strategies, it is apt to conclude with a little military thinking on the importance of judgement. In the British Army's *Guidelines for the Military Briefer*, Brigadier S. L. A. Marshall is quoted as defining the need for clarity of thought and concise judgement in expressing that thought. 'Battles are won through the ability of men to express concrete ideas in unmistakable language. All administration is carried forward along the chain of command by the power of men to make their thoughts articulate and available to others.' So, exercise your powers of judgement; they can be strengthened by exercise but, on the other hand, will become weak and flabby from disuse. By the same token, exercise your powers of expression. Thoughts, judgement, strategic concepts – none of them can become actions until articulated!

So, with this in mind, I have articulated the following 10 vital tips to help you as a strategist develop judgement and the effective ability to implement your strategies.

## Top 10 tips for strategists

1. Be focused in your aims. Use searching questions to analyse the situation and illuminate direction. Vigorous use of a strategic process model will ensure discipline of approach and control of outcomes.
2. Be creative and foster breakout thinking in other people. Think objectively about the power of the mind and the different forms creativity can take.
3. Value the power of the team – teams usually outperform the individual when it comes to creating new ideas and deciding how to implement them.
4. Be a change agent, develop a love of change without losing your perspective.
5. Appreciate that strategies must be led; so be a leader.
6. Value models of strategic analysis for the help they can give and the commercial perspective they add.
7. Embrace innovation as the key to progress and seek to develop organizational structures that encourage it.
8. Be persuasive, politically adept and streetwise in your dealings with others.
9. Be confident in yourself and in the value of the strategies you are seeking to implement – demonstrate that confidence in what you say and do.
10. Find a successful strategist as a tough role model – look to see what makes that person so good. Can you distil and bottle those talents for future use?

A tough agenda? Perhaps, but the latent strategist will devise a plan of learning and seek to develop his or her ability by actively seeking strategic opportunities to contribute to other people's strategies – at any stage of the process. There is only a small gap between learning and opportunism.

## Conclusion – a word of warning and hope

As we come to the end of this book, I feel that it is necessary to add a (light-hearted) word of warning. The techniques and tools that have been described here are the tools of change, improvement and progress – and regrettably there will always be opponents, those who feel threatened by the strategies thus conceived. The tools of questioning and analysis are tools that open minds and get their owners to see things differently. They are especially powerful and also seen by some as radically dangerous. Centuries ago, Socrates was put to death for the supposed crime of corrupting the young. His crime was, in fact, to say, 'Question everything'.

And what a potent message that is. The power of the simple question, no matter how naïve, has few boundaries. In Hans Andersen's fairy tale 'The King's New Clothes', it was the little boy who innocently asked why the King wore no clothes, thereby exposing both the frauds and the gullible people they had duped. Another philosopher, Aristotle, put a further perspective on the power of questions. When faced with an undesirable situation, he urged people to be 'restrained, questioning but not angry'. In fact, anger should not rule your actions; rather passion and enthusiasm.

And the purpose of good questions, as well as the worthwhile strategies to which they give birth, is to spread education, progress and improvement, no matter where or what the situation may be. Both are about learning how to see what needs to be seen and what needs to be done. As such, these strategies can themselves stretch out hands bearing knowledge, healing and hope in an often chaotic world.

# Bibliography

Barrett, G. (1995), *Forensic Marketing*, London, McGraw-Hill.

Bennis, W. (1989), *On Becoming a Leader*, Reading, MA, Addison-Wesley.

Blake, R. R. and J. S. Mouton (1994), *The Managerial Grid*, Houston, Texas, Gulf Publishing.

Blanchard, K. and S. Johnson (1983), *The One-minute Manager*, London, Fontana/Collins.

Bloom, A. (1987), *The Closing of the American Mind*, New York, Simon and Schuster.

Business Week (1997a), 'Damage Control – Can Mahathir get Malaysia back on course?', by M. Shari, B. Einhorn and S. Prasso in *Business Week*, 22 September.

Business Week (1997b), Statistics reported in *Business Week*, 15 December.

Business Week (1997c), 'Ikea's New Game Plan', by Julia Flynn and Lori Bongiorno in *Business Week*, 6 October.

Cadbury Report (1992), *The Cadbury Report on Corporate Governance*, London, Gee Publishing.

Campbell, D. (1985), *Take the Road to Creativity – and get off your dead end*, North Carolina, Centre for Creative Leadership.

Collins, J. C. and J. I. Porras (1996), 'Building Your Company's Vision', in *Harvard Business Review*, September–October.

Coyne, W. (1996), *The VR Innovation Lecture*, March 1996, London, Department of Trade and Industry.

Drucker, P. (1994), *Innovation and Entrepreneurship*, New York, Butterworth-Heinemann.

Eales-White, R. (1992), *The Power of Persuasion*, London, Kogan Page.

Eales-White, R. (1997), *Ask the Right Question*, Maidenhead, McGraw-Hill.

Gryskievicz, S. S. and D. A. Hills (1992), *Readings in Innovation*, North Carolina, Center for Creative Leadership.

Hamel, G. and C. Prahalad (1990), 'The Core Competence of the Corporation', in *Harvard Business Review*.

Hamel, G. and C. Prahalad (1993), 'Strategy as Stretch and Leverage', in *Harvard Business Review*, March–April.

Handy, C. (1988), *The Age of Unreason*, London, Business Books Ltd.

Harvey-Jones, J. (1994), *Making It Happen*, London, Harper–Collins.

Herrmann, N. (1988), *The Creative Brain*, North Carolina, Brain Books.

Herrmann, N. (1996), *The Whole Brain Business Book*, New York, McGraw-Hill.

Hersey, P. and K. H. Blanchard (1977), *Management of Organizational Behaviour: Utilizing Human Resources*, 3rd edition, Englewood Cliffs, NJ, Prentice-Hall.

IPD (1997), 'Proceedings of the IPD National Conference 1997'. Reported in *People Management*, 6 November.

Kao, J. (1996), *Jamming: The Art and Discipline of Business Creativity*, New York, Harper-Collins.

Kaplan, R. S. and D. P. Norton (1992), 'The Balanced Scorecard – Translating Strategy into Action – Measures that drive performance', in *Harvard Business Review*, January–February.

Kotter, J. (1990), *A Force for Change*, London, Collier MacMillan.

Labarre, P. (1997), 'This Organization is Disorganization', in *Fast Company*, Special Collector's Edition.

Lampikoski, C. and Emden, J. (1996), *Igniting Information,* Sussex, John Wiley.

McRae, H. (1994), *The World in 2020*, London, Harper-Collins.

Marshak, R. J. (1993), *Managing the Metaphors of Change*, USA, Organizational Dynamics.

Mintzberg, H. (1996), 'Musings on Management', in *Harvard Business Review*, July–August.

Naisbitt, J. (1994), *Global Paradox,* London, Nicholas Brealey.

Ohmae, K. (1983), *The Mind of the Strategist*, New York, Penguin Books.

Peters, T. J. and R. J. Waterman (1982), *In Search of Excellence*, New York, Harper and Row.

Peters, T. J. (1987), *Thriving on Chaos*, New York, Knopf.

Porter, M. (1985), *Competitive Advantage*, New York, The Free Press.

Pulley, M. L. (1997), 'Characteristics of Resilient People', in *Inklings*, the magazine of the Center for Creative Leadership, North Carolina, October.

Royal Society of Arts (1995), *Tomorrow's Company*, Aldershot, Gower Publishing.

Stewart, R. (1982), *Choices for the Manager*, London, McGraw-Hill.

Suarez, J. G. (1994), 'Managing Fear in the Workplace', *Journal for Quality and Participation*, December.

Toffler, A. (1973), *Future Shock*, London, Pan Books.

Treacy, M. and F. Wiersema (1995), *The Discipline of Market Leaders*, Reading, MA, Addison-Wesley.

van Maurik, J. (1994), *Discovering the Leader in You*, London, McGraw-Hill.

van Maurik, J. (1997), *The Portable Leader*, London, McGraw-Hill.

# Index